The Development of Greek Biography

The Development of Greek Biography

FOUR LECTURES *by Arnaldo Momigliano*

Harvard University Press   Cambridge, Massachusetts   1971

© Copyright 1971 by the President and Fellows of Harvard College
All rights reserved
Distributed in Great Britain by Oxford University Press, London
Library of Congress Catalog Card Number 73-139716
SBN 674-20040-3
Printed in the United States of America

To the memory of Isobel Henderson, scholar and friend

Preface

These four lectures are substantially published as they were delivered at Harvard University as the Carl Newell Jackson Classical Lectures in April 1968. Their aim is to provide an elementary but independent introduction to a difficult and important problem: the separation of biography and historiography. To my regret I could not do more within the packed schedule of my current commitments.

I am grateful to the colleagues and friends in the Department of the Classics at Harvard who invited me to deliver these lectures and received them with sympathy and constructive discussion. My debt to the generous hospitality and intellectual stimulus of Harvard has been enormously increased.

I am also grateful to the friends who, at a meeting of the Israel Academy of Jerusalem in October 1967 and at various sessions of my seminars in the Warburg Institute of London and in the Scuola Normale Superiore of Pisa, discussed earlier drafts of these lectures. Professor C. P. Jones (Toronto) read the manuscript twice and gave me the benefit of his exact scholarship and penetrating criticism. I owe other improvements to Professors H. Bloch and G. W. Bowersock.

Arnaldo Momigliano

Contents

The Development of Greek Biography

ABBREVIATIONS

FGrHist   *Die Fragmente der griechischen Historiker,* ed. F. Jacoby
IG   *Inscriptiones Graecae*
OGIS   *Orientis Graeci Inscriptiones Selectae*
POxy   *Oxyrhynchus Papyri*
RE   *Real-Encyclopädie der classischen Altertumswissenschaft,* ed. A. Pauly, G. Wissowa, et al.
RhM   *Rheinisches Museum für Philologie*
SGDI   *Sammlung der griechischen Dialekt-Inschriften,* ed. H. Collitz et al.

Introduction: The Ambiguous State of Biography

When I was young, scholars wrote history and gentlemen wrote biography. But were they gentlemen? Scholars were beginning to wonder. They were increasingly suspicious of their neighbours, the biographers. The biographers were no longer keeping in their place. They claimed to be endowed with special intuitions of human motives; they even claimed to be the real historians. The old and honoured distinction between history and biography—which Polybius (10.24) had proclaimed, Plutarch (*Alexander* 1.2) had recognized, and Eduard Meyer had reconfirmed as late as 1902—was apparently being denied by the boisterous international clan to which Emil Ludwig, André Maurois, and Lytton Strachey most conspicuously belonged. Dark forces loomed behind them. Did not Virginia Woolf suspect that human nature had changed in about December 1910? Scholars had not noticed the change, but biographers had seized upon it. Freud and Jung were opposing the subconscious motives of sex and death and the ancestral archetypes to the interpretation of history in terms of productive forces and cultural environment. The pupils of Stefan George despised progress and crowds and soon realized that biography rather than poetry was the natural medium of expression for their beliefs. In 1920 Friedrich Gundolf wrote the life of George himself, "der Gesamtmensch," along with Goethe and Napoleon a true ancient character—quite unlike Mommsen and Wilamowitz, "eingefleischte moderne Protestanten," "inveterate modern Protestants."

To tell the truth, the Hellenistic distinction between history and biography had been much less generally accepted than the example of Eduard Meyer seemed to show. Meyer's blunt statement, "aber eine eigentlich historische Tätigkeit ist sie [Biographie] nicht,"[1] was an exception even for its own time. In the leading handbooks on historical method which have been written since the sixteenth century, biography is normally regarded as one of the legitimate forms of historical writing. I shall give only one example for each century. Jean Bodin in his *Methodus ad facilem historiarum cognitionem* (1566) distinguished between the history of one man and that of a whole nation; he argued from Plutarch just as much as from Livy. A century later Agostino Mascardi in *Dell'arte historica* (1636) included "Vite" among the various divisions of history, the others being "Effemeridi," "Annali," "Cronache," "Commentari." In the eighteenth century l'Abbé de Mably accepted Plutarch as the model "historien des moeurs."[2]

In these three centuries the Hellenistic distinction between history and biography had been replaced by a rather uncontroversial recognition of biography as a type of history. No wonder that in the nineteenth century this seemed to be too simple a solution. When universal history was interpreted as the development of ideas, or of forms of production, what could the account of an individual life mean? Even a sensible and experienced historian like Johann Gustav Droysen found it difficult to rescue biography. In a remarkable paragraph of his lectures on *Historik* he made a distinction between men about whom one may write a biography and men about whom one may not. It would be mad, he contended, to try to write the biography of Caesar or of Frederick the Great: they belong to history. But Alcibiades, Cesare Borgia, Mirabeau—"das sind durch und durch biographische Figuren."[3] In other words, the adventurer, the failure, the marginal figure, were

[1] *Kleine Schriften* (1910) 66.
[2] *De la manière d'écrire l'histoire* (ed. 1784) 10.
[3] *Historik* (ed. 1937) 292.

the subjects for biography. J. Burckhardt would have disagreed: the discovery of biography and autobiography was for him an essential part of the discovery of man in the Italian Renaissance. But the distrust of biographers as expressed in Professor Bernheim's *Lehrbuch der historischen Methode* was more typical of prevailing opinion.

If the historians were so uncertain about what to leave to biographers, they could not complain if biographers claimed more and more from history. The biographers were backed by Burckhardt, by Nietzsche, by Freud, by Stefan George; they claimed to be supported by Athens and Rome, and at least had Bloomsbury behind them. Bertrand Russell was heard to laugh while reading *Eminent Victorians* in His Majesty's gaol, where he was confined as a pacifist writer in 1918. Mussolini arranged to have Emil Ludwig as his Eckermann. The previous hagiography by his lover Margherita Sarfatti was no longer enough for him. When Giovanni Papini became a convert, he announced his conversion to the world in a life of Christ written in the Emil Ludwig style. German professors collectively protested in emotional pages of the *Historische Zeitschrift* against what they called "Historische Belletristik." A relative of Theodor Mommsen wrote a discourse against Emil Ludwig. Robin Collingwood, who was very sensitive to anything Bloomsbury thought and said, reacted by reiterating Eduard Meyer's condemnation of all biography: "Of everything other than thought, there can be no history. Thus a biography, for example, however much history it contains, is constructed on principles that are not only non-historical but anti-historical."[4] Benedetto Croce more calmly reminded his readers that "writers such as Ludwig are the Guido da Veronas of historiography,"[5] Guido da Verona being a half-sentimental, half-pornographic minor novelist of the 'twenties. But Croce's theoretical position was less clear than his joke assumed. Though a keen writer of biographies himself, he had put forward many ideas

[4] *The Idea of History*, 304.
[5] *Storia della storiografia italiana nel sec. XIX* II, 3rd ed., 282.

that were bound to shake any faith in the possibility of biography. In literary criticism—witness his books on Dante and Shakespeare—he had made a sharp distinction between the biographical data and the artistic personality of a writer: the former were irrelevant to the latter. In general history he had emphasized that events, not intentions, were what counted. More radically he had denied that individuals exist: what exists, according to him, is the Universal Spirit. If Croce had been consistent, he would have denied biography any right to exist, as Collingwood had done.

As it happens, I belong to a family which was given to biographical writing in the early part of this century. The degree of sophistication and of scholarly responsibility of these biographies was high. Felice Momigliano's many biographical essays on figures of the Italian Risorgimento never amounted to full-scale biographies, but at least one of them, the psychological comparison between Mazzini and Cattaneo, was a pioneer work when it appeared in 1901. Felice Momigliano was incidentally also a biographer of Tolstoi and a major intellectual influence on his friend Luigi Pirandello. Attilio Momigliano's monograph on Manzoni, which appeared in two parts in 1915 and 1919, has of course become a classic of Italian literary criticism. The little book on Crispi by another member of my family, A. C. Jemolo, revealed an uncommon sensitiveness to psychological complexities and moral issues. The use as early as 1922 of such psychological methods in the study of one of the most controversial Italian politicians was bold and disturbing.

Felice Momigliano died in 1924, too early to be affected by the new situation. Attilio Momigliano and Arturo Carlo Jemolo stopped writing biographical works. What was a major international crisis in the writing of history became a domestic crisis in my family circle. Eucardio Momigliano, a lawyer whose successful political career had been interrupted by Fascism, published books which seemed to be dangerously inspired by Maurois and Ludwig. They were translated into five or six foreign languages and are still being reprinted now after forty years: they have certainly proved their right to exist. But they seemed extremely embarrassing at the time— almost a betrayal of family standards.

This, perhaps, can explain my own attitude towards biographical work in my early years. Though extremely interested in the study of personality, I was anxious to avoid mere biographical detail in my youthful monographs on Claudius and Philip of Macedon. Political and cultural problems, not individuals, were my business then. In those distant days I did make a keen study of ancient biography too. As early as 1928 I studied the only surviving biographer of the Hellenistic period, Satyrus, and reviewed D. R. Stuart's *Epochs of Greek and Roman Biography*. A little later I wrote the articles on Plutarch and Suetonius for the Italian Encyclopaedia. But soon I turned away from ancient biography. I must recognize in retrospect that for thirty-five years, if not longer, I seem to have tried hard to avoid being enmeshed in the serious and diverse questions that surround ancient biography.

If now, in my old age, I come back to ancient biography, it is not so much in repentance as in the realization that what in my youth was the most difficult branch of history is now the easiest. Biography has never been so popular, so respected, so uncontroversial, among scholars as it is now. Even the palmy days of the eighteenth century, when Plutarch was the master, are nothing in comparison with the present popularity of biography among historians in general and ancient historians in particular. This unanimity extends to Marxist historians. Who would have expected to see Plutarch becoming the darling of the true Marxist–Leninist historian? Yet S. S. Averincev and other Russian scholars have been writing not only competently, but enthusiastically, about Plutarch in the *Vestnik Drevnej Istorii* and elsewhere in recent years.

There are several reasons for the new popularity of biography. It is partly due to the diversification of modern biography into various types which satisfy different needs. The traditional cultural historian can still derive infinite pleasure from masterpieces of the old type such as Werner

Kaegi's monumental biography of Burckhardt. The psycho-
analyst has of course his Erikson, and the ex-Marxist can turn
to the theory, if not to the practice, of Roy Pascal. Biography
by the thousand—what we ancient historians call prosopog-
raphy and the modern historians, at least in England, call
"namierization of history"—provides the social historians
with new material. What is perhaps more important is the
negative fact that full-blooded social history is becoming more
and more intractable owing to its increasing refinements and
complications. Anyone who follows with admiration the
activities of the Sixième Section of the École des Hautes
Études wonders whether such a microscopic analysis of social
developments can be pursued indefinitely. Will the historians
ever be able to number the innumerable facets of life? In this
situation of uncertainty, a biography at least seems to represent something circumscribed. Whatever objection we ancient
historians may have against the prosopographical approach
to Roman politics, at least it does provide firm data: careers
and family connections are facts. Biography has acquired
an ambiguous role in historical research: it may be a tool
of social research or it may be an escape from social
research.

Nobody nowadays is likely to doubt that biography is
some kind of history. We may well turn back to the inventors
of biography, the ancient Greeks, to ask why they never
recognized that biography is history. We may also ask some
other questions which spring directly from the new situation
of biography in contemporary historiography. We may ask
what was the position of autobiography in relation to biography in the ancient world: the same question exists for
twentieth-century historiography. We may ask what was the
part of philosophy in shaping the forms of ancient biography:
the same question of course exists for modern biography, as
Wilhelm Dilthey was the first to explain.

The new privileged position of biography in contemporary
historical studies is in itself a paradox which invites questions
—and doubts. We can extend our questions and clarify our

doubts if we study the history of biography in its development and in its changing relations to historiography. In these lectures I can offer only a few facts and a few suggestions concerning the origins of the imposing phenomenon of biography. I shall at least try not to avoid difficulties and not to conceal ignorance, whether it is my personal ignorance or lack of evidence.

I Modern Theories on Ancient Biography

I

The first fact we have to face in surveying ancient Greek and Latin biography is that our information about it is very uneven. We are especially ignorant about the period of its origins in the fifth and fourth centuries B.C. and about the period of the most learned research in biography of the third and second centuries B.C. This means that the situation regarding ancient biography (leaving aside the Near East for the moment) is different from that regarding ancient political historiography. We possess some of the basic classics of the political historiography of the fifth and fourth centuries B.C. —Herodotus, Thucydides, Xenophon, though we have lost Hellanicus, Ephorus, and Theopompus. But we have none of the biographical and autobiographical literature of the fifth century and have to rely on Isocrates' *Euagoras* and Xenophon's *Agesilaus,* which describe themselves as encomia, and on a philosophic novel, Xenophon's *Cyropaedia,* for some aspects of biography in the fourth century. The loss of the original biographical writings of the third century B.C.—with the only exception of a fragment of Satyrus' life of Euripides recovered from an Oxyrhynchus papyrus in 1912—is matched by the almost total loss of the general historiography of the third century, including Hieronymus of Cardia, the historian of the successors of Alexander the Great, and Timaeus of Tauromenium, the historian of the West. But the fact that we are reasonably well informed about the work of historians of the fourth century and that we can pick up the thread again with Polybius in the second century makes the loss of the general historiography of the third century less disastrous. There is no extant biography of the second century B.C. to perform the same service on the biographical side.

The first collection of biographies we possess is by Cornelius Nepos, a contemporary of Cicero and a writer in Latin. Next comes Nicolaus of Damascus; the fragments of his life of Augustus and of his autobiography are preserved coherently and authentically enough to represent, next to Satyrus, the earliest examples of Hellenistic biography and autobiography to have been directly transmitted to us. Nicolaus of Damascus is also the earliest writer known to have written in succession a universal history, a biography, and an autobiography. The activity of Hellenistic *érudits* in preparing biographies of poets, orators, philosophers, and so on, is known to us almost exclusively through later summaries, compilations, and scholia. All the monographs about kings which were common in the Hellenistic period are entirely lost, including the earliest histories of Alexander the Great and works on such promising subjects as "Lives of those who passed from philosophy to tyranny and despotic rule" by the third-century writer Hermippus.

Broadly speaking, the only period of ancient biography which we know from direct acquaintance with the original works is the period of the Roman Empire. The first names that occur to us in speaking of ancient biography—Plutarch, Suetonius, Diogenes Laertius, Philostratus, the *Scriptores Historiae Augustae*—all belong to the Imperial age. Furthermore, it is clear that biography became far more important in the period after Constantine. Pagan philosophers and sophists and Christian saints and martyrs, the main subjects of late Roman biography, are suited even less than the heroes of the early Roman Empire to give a clear idea of Greek and Hellenistic biographies. There was of course considerable continuity in technique and content between Hellenistic and late Roman biography. But late Roman biography reflects an age of conversion; and A. D. Nock has taught us to regard conversion as a new feature of the Christian centuries.

II

Modern scholars have tried in various ways to overcome the paucity of information about the early history of biography. Source criticism as exemplified by Wilamowitz's *Antigonos von Karystos* has undoubtedly contributed to the recognition of Hellenistic materials in later compilations. Following Wilamowitz, his pupil and rival Eduard Schwartz produced a model analysis of the sources of Diogenes Laertius in his article in Pauly–Wissowa. But neither Wilamowitz nor Schwartz ever attempted to give a general characterization of Hellenistic biography or to write a history of its antecedents. It was Friedrich Leo who tried to define the basic forms of Hellenistic biography, whereas Ivo Bruns studied the development of the characterization of individuals in pre-Hellenistic literature, and G. Misch attempted a general history of Greek and Roman autobiography. More recently A. Dihle has tried to trace the origins of Greek biography to Socrates and the Socratics. Leo, Bruns, and Misch are three great names, and their works on ancient historical literature are among the great achievements of German scholarship of the Wilamowitz era. I for one shall never forget the impression their works made on me when I first read them as an undergraduate forty years ago. The work by Dihle, though of a different class and belonging to a different age, still has its uses. But it is urgent to re-examine the very basis on which these scholars have erected their constructions. I think the best way to do this is to formulate independently the most obvious questions suggested by the extant evidence on biography and to see to what extent these questions differ from those asked by Bruns, Misch, Leo, and Dihle.

III

An account of the life of a man from birth to death is what I call biography. This is not a very profound definition, but it has the advantage of excluding any discussion of how biography should be written. It is not for a historian of biography to decide what biography should be, though he may have his preferences. It may be true, as William Roscoe Thayer suggested in *The Art of Biography* (1920), that the "constant direction in the evolution of biography has been from the outward to the inward," but this is a hypothesis which needs verification. What matters more to our purpose is that our definition leaves us free to study the prehistory of biography, the formative elements of this new literary genre. It may be objected that, fortunately or unfortunately, nobody has ever succeeded in giving, or perhaps even attempted, a complete account of what one man did during his lifetime. But this seems to be the paradoxical character of biography: it must always give *partem pro toto*; it must always achieve completeness by selectiveness. I must add that it seems very doubtful to me whether incompleteness is, as some would maintain, characteristic of all historical accounts, biographical or otherwise. I believe I can formulate historical themes in which the historian has no need to be selective in his account of the relevant facts and may even have the obligation of not being selective. A piece of historical research intended to establish what books Dante wrote must and can be exhaustive within its terms of reference. But since any biography is inevitably selective we cannot separate biography from autobiography which is the account of a life written by the man who is living it: unless you believe in spiritualism or in prophecy, autobiographies can never include the whole life from birth to death. But autobiographies can, like ordinary biographies, be so directed as to represent a whole life. In the classical world we must also bear in mind that Greeks and Romans wrote about gods and heroes who were born but did not die, or at least died a death which was only the beginning of a new period of activity. We may ultimately choose to leave aside lives of gods and heroes in so far as they are lives of non-existing beings. But we cannot exclude a priori that biographies of gods and heroes preceded and influenced the biographies of men.

The first question is the date of the most ancient Greek biographies and autobiographies. This will have to be answered in detail later. But at this stage we can suggest that attempts at biographical writing were made in the fifth century B.C.

Professor H. Homeyer in a very valuable paper in *Philologus* 1962 has shown that Herodotus includes several biographies. Her contention that the Greeks knew biography in the fifth century can be supported by other data.

This raises our second question. It is obviously no mere coincidence that biography came into being at approximately the same time as general historiography. On the other hand, biography was never considered as history in the classical world. The relationship between history and biography varied in different periods. We have to account both for their separation and for their changing relations. This, incidentally, may lead to a more rigorous interpretation of Aristotle's statement that "a particular fact" is what Alcibiades did or what was done to him (*Poetics* 9).

Thirdly, though we hear of biographies, and perhaps of autobiographies, as early as the fifth century B.C., biography became a precise notion and got an appropriate word only in the Hellenistic age. The word is *bios*—not *biographia,* which first appears in fragments of Damascius' *Life of Isidorus* (end of the fifth century A.D.) preserved by Photius (ninth century) in his *Bibliotheca* 181 and 242. We must therefore account for the Hellenistic clarification of the notion of biography. This includes a study of the relation between *bios* and *encomium* in Hellenistic theory and practice.

Fourthly, we must not assume a priori that *bios* invariably meant the description of an individual life as such, of a man in so far as he differs from all other men. The notion of personality is certainly found in modern European languages, but I doubt whether there is an adequate translation of it into ancient Greek. To stick to elementary facts, it gives us something to think about that Hellenistic and Roman biographers often wrote series of biographies of men of the same type—generals, philosophers, demagogues—and therefore seem to have cared for the type rather than for the individual.

Fifthly, the Greeks distinguished between history and erudition, between what they called *historia* and what they called less clearly and less unequivocally *archaeologia* or *philologia* and the Romans translated as *antiquitates*. The distinction was by no means sharp and self-evident, but it did exist, and I was able to trace its development in an old lecture of mine at the Warburg Institute.[1] The basic distinction between the two subjects was that history dealt mainly with political and military events and was written in a chronological order, whereas erudition dealt with almost anything else —from personal names to religious ceremonies—and preferred systematic survey to chronological order. It follows that it is not enough to try to define the relations between history and biography in the Greek and Roman sense of the words. We have also to ask what is the relation between biography and erudition. The question is worth asking. *Bios* was not a word reserved for the life of an individual man. It was also used for the life of a country. In Hellenistic and Roman times there existed works, such as βίος ʽΕλλάδος (life of Greece), *vita populi romani* (life of the Roman people), of an indisputably antiquarian character. Furthermore, we know that biography developed in the Hellenistic age in conjunction with philological commentaries and surveys, such as the Callimachean *pinakes*: here we are faced by a close connection between biography and philology. But the most important fact to be examined is that ancient biographies did not necessarily follow a chronological order; nor is chronological order

---

[1] Now in my *Studies in Historiography* (1966) 1–35.

a necessary feature even of modern biographies. There is a characteristic type of ancient biography which Leo has taught us to identify with Suetonius; prima facie it presents formal resemblances to the systematic structure of erudite works.

Sixthly and finally, we have to face again the uncertainties and ambiguities of the relationship between biography and autobiography. If biography is an ancient Greek word, though of late antiquity, autobiography is not a Greek word but a modern invention. According to the *O.E.D.* it first appeared in English in 1809 with Robert Southey. The facts known to me seem to point to a more interesting origin. In 1796 Isaac D'Israeli devoted a chapter of his *Miscellanies or Literary Recreations* to "Some observations on diaries, self-biography and self-characters" (pages 95–110). The reviewer of D'Israeli's book in the *Monthly Review* 24 (1797) 375 noticed the word *self-biography* and commented: "We are doubtful whether the latter word be legitimate . . . yet *auto-biography* would have seemed pedantic." The anonymous writer in the *Monthly Review* seems to have invented the word *autobiography*. Though pedantic it proved to be preferable to *self-biography*, which D'Israeli had favoured. The *Wörterbuch* by the Brothers Grimm did not register this word in German in 1853. The *Grand Dictionnaire Universel Larousse* declared in 1866 that "ce mot, quoique d'origine grecque, est de fabrique anglaise." The nearest approximation in Ancient Greek is περὶ τοῦ ἰδίου βίου καὶ τῆς ἑαυτοῦ ἀγωγῆς, which is the title of the autobiography of Nicolaus of Damascus in the *Suda*. The title is undoubtedly authentic because it corresponds to the title *De vita sua* which some Romans gave to their own memoirs in the Republican period (for instance, M. Aemilius Scaurus, consul 115, P. Rutilius). It shows that at least in the late Hellenistic period and in the early Roman Empire an autobiographical work belonged to the category of *bioi, vitae*—in other words it was treated as biography.

But the letters, speeches, commentaries (ὑπομνήματα, *commentarii*), and accounts of journeys performed functions which can only be called autobiographical. We shall try to go into these works which certainly preceded the appearance of full-fledged autobiographies. Wilamowitz and Leo denied that the Greeks knew autobiography. Leo wrote: "In dieser Neigung des griechischen Geistes zum Typischen liegt der Grund, warum die Griechen keine Autobiographie besassen."[2] I wonder whether Leo could have written in this way if he had taken into account the extensive Greek autobiographical material outside the formal *bios*. One important question connected with the relations between biography and autobiography is whether an ancient writer was expected to be more objective, more careful in his facts, less inclined to praise and blame, when he wrote about somebody else's life than when he wrote about himself. Here again we must beware of modern ways of thinking. Autobiography is now the most subjective kind of self-expression. We expect confessions, rather than factual information, in autobiographies, whereas we expect factual information rather than subjective effusions in biography. The most elementary facts about ancient biographical and autobiographical writing are a warning that this may not have been so in Greece and Rome. There was a close relation, if nothing more, between *bios* and *encomium*. On the other hand autobiographical commentaries were often written for the direct purpose of being used as raw materials by historians. Whereas biographers were free to be encomiastic, autobiographers seem to have been bound to be factual—at least in certain cases.

Thus six essential problems have emerged: (1) What is the date of the most ancient Greek biographies and autobiographies? (2) What was the relation between history and biography in the classical world? (3) How did the notion of *bios* become formalized in the Hellenistic age? (4) How did autobiography develop in relation to biography? (5) What was the relation between the notion of an individual *bios* and the notion of a collective *bios*? (6) Within what limits did biography belong to erudition rather than to history? Other

---

[2] *Geschichte der röm. Literatur* I (1913) 342.

problems remained in the background but can now easily be added. For instance: What was the particular contribution, if any, of the Romans to the development of classical biography and autobiography? Or again (though this theme will not even be alluded to in the following lectures): Exactly what changed in biography and autobiography when the Christians took over?

These questions only partially coincide with those formulated by Bruns, Leo, Misch, and Dihle. I shall examine Dihle after Bruns and Leo after Misch for reasons which will become immediately apparent. Ivo Bruns, as is well known, published *Das literarische Porträt der Griechen im fünften und vierten Jahrhundert vor Christi Geburt* in 1896 and supplemented it with the shorter essay *Die Persönlichkeit in der Geschichtsschreibung der Alten* in 1898. The purpose of the first volume, to put it very simply, was to discover how Attic writers described and appreciated individuals. In the second book, perhaps even more significant than the first, Bruns developed the thesis that there are historians like Thucydides and Livy who characterize an individual indirectly, whereas there are others, such as Xenophon in the *Anabasis* and Polybius, who express their opinions about historical personalities by direct characterization and judgements. While Livy never said what he thought about Scipio Africanus but grouped the facts so as to convey an impression, Polybius was direct in his judgement of Scipio. Though Bruns admitted exceptions in Livy (for instance, in the famous direct characterization of Cato in book 39), he concluded that annalistic writers, such as Thucydides and Livy, preferred indirect characterization, whereas writers of monographs, biographies, and autobiographies adopted the direct method. Bruns had been impressed by Burckhardt and wanted to see whether the ancient world knew and appreciated the individual, as the Renaissance, according to Burckhardt, had done. The question, though not out of place, was too vague in one direction and too precise in another. It was too vague because Bruns never tackled the problem of the origins of either biography or autobiography, though they were well within his chronological limits. Given the impor-

tance which Burckhardt attributed to biography and autobiography in the Renaissance discovery of man, this is surprising. From another point of view, the question Bruns
asked was too precise. As I have already hinted, we have no
reason to believe that "literarisches Porträt," "Individuali-
tät," "Persönlichkeit," and so forth, are terms which can be
transferred to the Greek and Roman world without a great
deal of explaining—even of explaining away.

I put Dihle next to Bruns because I feel that something of
Bruns's attitude towards the problem of Greek individualism
has passed into Dihle's with a touch of Gundolf in addition.
Dihle assumed that a great personality was needed to inspire the invention of biography and thought he had found
this personality in Socrates. The Socratics collected the traits
of Socrates' personality, and finally the Peripatos formalized
biography. Now our evidence, as we shall see later, seems to
point to the conclusion that biography and autobiography
existed one hundred years before Socrates' death. Nor do we
know that any Socratic, Aristotle included, ever wrote the
life of Socrates. The extant apologies by Plato and Xenophon
and Xenophon's *Memorabilia* can certainly not be overlooked
in a history of biography. But they are not full biographies,
and there were apologies and probably recollections by writers
who lived earlier than Socrates or were remote from the
Socratic schools. Dihle was certainly right in emphasizing the
importance of the Socratic schools in the development of
biography and autobiography. My own researches will support his contention. But neither did Socrates inspire the
invention of biography, nor were the Socratics responsible
for the most momentous developments in the art of biography. Concern with modern presuppositions is even more
obvious in Misch's *Geschichte der Autobiographie*, the first
volume of which appeared in 1907 and was immediately
greeted by Wilamowitz as a masterpiece.[3] Misch revised and

---

[3] It is interesting to compare Wilamowitz' review in *Internat. Wochenschrift
für Wissenschaft* 1 (1907) 1105–1114 with F. Jacoby's review in *Deutsche Literaturzeitung* 30 (1909) 1093 and 1157. Later W. Jaeger commented on Misch's
second version in *Speculum* 28 (1953) 405–410, reprinted in *Scripta Minora* II
(1960) 455–462.

largely rewrote this book when he was a refugee in England during the Second World War, but we must go back to the first edition for the true flavour of the ideas which inspired him. Misch was the pupil and son-in-law of W. Dilthey and his definition of autobiography as a "history of human self-awareness"[4] is clearly influenced by Dilthey. Consequently Misch did not confine himself to what we would call autobiographical works: he tried even less to decide whether we are entitled to draw a line between true autobiographies, memoirs of one's own times, diaries, etc. He examined any piece of poetry and prose which contained personal elements, whatever their nature and whatever their purpose. He included Cicero's and Seneca's letters and gave pride of place to Marcus Aurelius' εἰς ἑαυτόν, though he knew that the latter are not autobiographical except in the first book and belong to the literary genre of the *soliloquia*. The result is something of considerable interest in so far as it clarifies what the ancients felt about themselves, but is confusing as a history of autobiography. Caesar's *Commentarii* are autobiographical (at least to a large extent), but hardly a document of self-awareness. Flavius Josephus' autobiography, the oldest we possess in its original form, is plainly written in self-defense. The first work which combines autobiographical information and self-awareness perfectly is of course St. Augustine's *Confessions*. But this means that Misch's *History of Ancient Autobiography*, as history of self-awareness, ends where it should begin.

F. Leo's *Die griechisch-römische Biographie nach ihrer literarischen Form* (1901) is a less exciting, but perhaps more lasting, performance. Leo started from Suetonius and Plutarch and made it clear that they represent two different types of biography. The Suetonian type is the combination of a tale in chronological order with the systematic characterization of an individual and of his achievements. As such it is naturally well suited to lives of writers. The Plutarchean type

---

[4] *History of Autobiography* I (1950) 8.

is a straightforward chronological account of events and as such is well suited to tell the life of a general or of a politician. It was Leo's opinion that the Plutarchean type of biography was invented by early Peripatetics to tell the story of states-men, whereas the Suetonian type was introduced by Alexan-drian grammarians under the influence of Aristotelian teaching. It was first used to write the lives of artists and writers. Again according to Leo, Suetonius, who was pri-marily a grammarian, used this type to write lives not only of literary men but also of Roman emperors.

Criticism has grown against Leo's reconstruction of the history of biography. In 1927 W. Uxkull-Gyllenband made a rather weak attempt to prove that the Plutarchean type of biography had been inspired not by Aristotle, but by Panae-tius and Posidonius.[5] Neither Panaetius nor Posidonius is known to have written biographies, though Panaetius dis-cussed biographical details within the context of his great book on philosophic sects. In 1931 A. Weizsäcker[6] and in 1951 W. Steidle[7] tried to deny or to reduce the importance of Leo's analysis of the two basic biographical forms. Weiz-säcker observed that even the Plutarchean type was not entirely organized in chronological order—which is true—and concluded that therefore it is not essentially different from the Suetonian type—which does not follow. Steidle, in a more complex analysis of certain features of Suetonius' biographies, tried to indicate what is peculiarly Roman in them and dismissed as of secondary importance or irrelevant the formal features which Leo had considered significant. When Steidle pointed out that Suetonius judges Roman emperors according to Roman values, he was of course right, though perhaps not surprisingly so. But he was not justified in concluding that Suetonius' *Caesars* are less far removed from ordinary political historiography than Plutarch's heroes. What remains true in Leo's classification is the demonstration

[5] *Plutarch und die griechische Biographie.*
[6] *Untersuchungen über Plutarchs biographische Technik.*
[7] *Sueton und die antike Biographie.*

that Suetonius was under the influence of an antiquarian approach to biography, whereas Plutarch was nearer to political historiography. Other critics of Leo, such as N. I. Barbu,[8] have rather perversely emphasized Plutarch's right to be considered a historian—which is not what Plutarch claimed to be.

The real question raised by Leo's book is whether we are right in placing on the school of Aristotle the burden of having invented biography. Leo was of course familiar with most of the evidence which would point to an earlier date for some Greek biographies, but he was somehow fascinated by the obscurity which surrounds the earliest generations of the Peripatetic school. There are enough indications that the early Peripatetics collected biographical material, wrote definite biographies, and generally stimulated what we call Alexandrian scholarship. But anyone who reads Leo's chapters on the Peripatos carefully will have to admit that Leo sees Aristotle as an ancient Mommsen urging his pupils to do what he had no time to do himself and creating the conditions for new branches of learning to develop. This says much for the vitality of the German academic ideal from Leibniz through Humboldt and Niebuhr to Mommsen and his pupils, of whom Leo liked to consider himself one. *Organisation der wissenschaftlichen Arbeit* is the title of a famous paper by Hermann Usener on the Academy and the Peripatos (1884) with which Leo was well acquainted.[9] "So ist die griechische Wissenschaft geschaffen worden, das Werk, wie wir nun sehen, von zwei Generationen, genau genommen von zwei Männern, Platon und Aristoteles, das Ergebnis einer wunderbaren Organisation der geistigen Arbeit" ("Thus Greek science was created, the work, as we now see, of two generations, more precisely of two men, Plato and Aristotle, the result of a wonderful organization of intellectual work"). The

---

[8] *Les procédés de la peinture des caractères et la vérité historique dans les biographies de Plutarque*, 1934.

[9] *Vorträge und Aufsätze*, 2nd ed., Leipzig-Berlin 1914, 67–102 = *Preussische Jahrbücher* 53 (1884) 1–25.

idea that biography and autobiography might have been born among scatterbrained Ionian sailors or among dubious dilettanti and sophists was not likely to appeal to the great men who, quite rightly, saw themselves as the continuators of the Aristotelian tradition in learning.

Burckhardt, Dilthey, Stefan George, Mommsen (or rather Mommsen's vision of an ideal Academy) have so far conditioned research on Greek biography. Bruns was inspired by Burckhardt, Misch by Dilthey, Dihle by Stefan George, Leo by Usener and Mommsen.

It becomes clear, therefore, that the question of chronology is of paramount importance in the evaluation of the history of ancient biography. Duane Reed Stuart was perhaps aware of this point when he gave his Sather Lectures, *Epochs of Greek and Roman Biography* (1928). But his was only a half-hearted attempt to seek the origins of Greek biography in the fifth century B.C. As I have said above, we owe to Professor Homeyer a far more precise analysis of some of the evidence involved.[10]

I think I can add a few other facts to those collected by Professor Homeyer. But I should like above all to try to direct attention to the complex origin of Greek historical research in the fifth century as exemplified by the birth of biography. Curiosity was a far more powerful motive in determining the oldest form of historical research than modern scholars are prepared to admit. Herodotus would have nodded his assent to Catherine Drinker Bowen's dictum: "History is in its essence exciting."[11] In 1934 Mark Longaker observed acutely, "The present day reader most often goes to biography because he is interested in himself."[12] This does not necessarily apply to ancient readers. I suspect that at first the Greek reader did not go to biography because he was interested in himself. He wanted to know about heroes, poets, unusual men, such as kings and tyrants. He liked

[10] *Philologus* 106 (1962) 75–85.
[11] *The Writing of Biography* (1950) 3.
[12] *Contemporary Biography*, 11.

biographies just as much as he liked foreign lands. Later, however, there were also in Greece readers who took to biography as a mirror of human nature. Biography did not necessarily become more concerned with the things of the spirit, but it became more ambitious.

II Fifth-Century Biographies and Autobiographies?

I

The question of what we may properly regard as the antecedents of fully developed biography and autobiography of the Hellenistic period is one that does not admit of a clear-cut answer. Any account in verse or prose that tells us something about an individual can be taken as preparatory to biography; and any statement about onself, whether in poetry or in prose, can be regarded as autobiographical. Looked at from this angle, the whole of the surviving epic and lyric poetry of the Greeks is antecedent either to biography or to autobiography.[1] But it seems reasonable to restrict the search for the antecedents of biography to works or sections of works whose explicit purpose is to give some account of an individual in isolation (instead of treating him as one of the many actors in a historical event). Similarly, I shall look for the antecedents of autobiography among accounts, however partial, of the writer's past life rather than among expressions of his present state of mind. In other words I incline to take anecdotes, collections of sayings, single or collected letters, and apologetic speeches as the truest antecedents of either biography or autobiography.

---

[1] The existence of specifically autobiographic poems is doubtful. Xenophanes frag. 18 Diehl[2] = 22 Diels[6] may be the beginning of such an autobiography (H. Fränkel, *Dichtung und Philosophie des frühen Griechentums* [2nd ed. 1962] 372). Yet cf. M. Untersteiner, *Senofane* (1955) 134.

Let me, however, first of all indicate a few factors which might have contributed to the origins of Greek biography but in all likelihood did not. We can take it for granted that the Greeks, like other nations, had funeral orations and songs in honour of the dead—all of which are potential biographies. The *Iliad* presents the ceremonial laments of Andromache, Hecuba, and Helen over the dead body of Hector (24.720). Pre-Solonian Athens is credited with the custom of funeral speeches in praise of the dead (Cicero *De legibus* 2.63). The chorus in Aeschylus expects somebody to sing the praise of the dead Agamemnon (*Agamemnon* 1548). There is no evidence that anything like a biography evolved directly from these ceremonial performances. But in the fourth century B.C. Isocrates shaped his encomium of Euagoras in the form of a commemorative speech: he exploited an occasion, if not a tradition.

Greek aristocracy shared the passion for genealogical trees which characterizes any aristocracy. As we know from Hecataeus of Miletus, it was no extravagance to claim fifteen ancestors. The genealogy of the great clan of the Philaidai, as reported by Pherecydes of Athens (*FGrHist* 3F2), and the famous inscription of Heropythos of Chios[2] show that in the fifth century in Greece quite a few families, apart from the Spartan kings, produced genealogies going back to the eighth or ninth century B.C. But this interest in genealogy does not seem to have produced a corresponding interest in biography. If we are to judge by Hecataeus, he told stories about himself, not about his ancestors. The Roman aristocrats of the third and second centuries B.C. knew, or at least spoke, more about their ancestors of the fifth century than the Greek aristocrats of the fifth century spoke about theirs of two or three centuries before.

But the Greeks had a long-standing interest in heroes of the past—Heracles, Theseus, Oedipus—and this is directly rele-

---

[2] *SGDI* 5656. For the date, L. H. Jeffery, *The Local Scripts of Archaic Greece* (1961) 344.

vant to the origins of biography. Poems told episodes of their lives. In the early fifth century B.C. prose works replaced or supplemented poetry in this kind of mythical biography. To take the simplest example, Theocritus believed that Pisander of Camyrus was the first of the poets of old "to record for you the son of Zeus, the lion-slayer prompt of hand, and all the labors he accomplished" (*Epigrammata* 22; transl. A. S. F. Gow). The epic poet Pisander can hardly have lived after 550 B.C.[3] He was, no doubt, used by the prose writer Pherecydes of Athens, who seems to have been active in the first quarter of the fifth century B.C., though the demonstration provided by F. Jacoby for this date is not so strong as he believed.[4] We may assume the same type of relationship between the poem *Theseis*, probably of the late sixth century B.C., and the corresponding section of Pherecydes. The new interest in the lives of heroes is also reflected in late archaic art. The sequence of the deeds of Theseus in the Treasury of the Athenians at Delphi has been defined a "*bios* of the hero in chronological order."[5]

Furthermore, curiosity surrounded the personalities of the ancient poets such as Homer and Hesiod. At least Hesiod provided autobiographical details which later poets imitated. His encounter with the Muses became a commonplace to be found with appropriate variants in Parmenides, Callimachus, Ennius, Propertius, and others. Speculations about the lives of Homer and Hesiod are certainly earlier than the fifth century B.C.

Heraclitus refers to a story about the death of Homer as common knowledge (frag. 56). According to Tatianus, Theagenes of Rhegium, who lived before 500 B.C., did research on the life of Homer (Diels, *Vorsokratiker* I 51).[6]

[3] R. Keydell, *RE* s.v. "Peisandros," 144; Wilamowitz, *Textgesch. d. griech. Lyriker,* 66 n. 1.

[4] F. Jacoby, *Abhandl. zur griechischen Geschichtschreibung* (1956) 116; H. T. Wade-Gery, *The Poet of the Iliad* (1952) 90.

[5] G. M. A. Hanfmann, "Narration in Greek Art," *American Journal of Archaeology* 61 (1957) 73.

[6] R. Pfeiffer, *History of Classical Scholarship* (1968) 11; cf. R. Cantarella, *Parola del Passato* 112 (1967) 1–28.

Research—or imagination—about the lives of Homer and Hesiod was intensified in the fifth century. The clan of the Homeridae who rather dubiously claimed descent from Homer through a daughter of the poet may have contributed to the formation of the fifth-century legends about the two poets. Learned men collected previous traditions and drew inferences from the poems themselves. Even Thucydides took an interest in such biographical details. He tells us that in 426 the Athenian strategos Demosthenes camped with his army "in the precinct of Nemean Zeus, where the poet Hesiod is said to have been killed by the men of that region, an oracle having told him that he should suffer this fate at Nemea" (3.96).

The publication of Papyrus Michigan 2754 in 1925 at last proved that Nietzsche had been right after all in attributing the authorship of the so-called *Agon* between Homer and Hesiod to the sophist Alcidamas who lived about 400 B.C. The text transmitted by the Byzantine tradition has interpolations not earlier than Hadrian. The fact that E. Meyer[7] and Wilamowitz[8] were among the opponents of Nietzsche who were shown to be wrong by Papyrus Michigan has its amusing side—the more so because Meyer had acutely perceived that Aristophanes, *Peace* 1282–1283, alluded to an episode to be found also in the *Agon*. Meyer implicitly recognized that the author of the *Agon* had worked on material circulating in the second part of the fifth century B.C.

There is nothing surprising in the conclusion of the *Agon*: the victory of Hesiod over Homer. Hesiod in his *Works and Days* had boasted of his victory in Chalcis but had left his rivals unnamed. When the biographers chose to make Homer the rival of Hesiod in order to establish that there had been contact between them, they had to take the consequence and accept that Hesiod had had the best of Homer. The personal contribution of Alcidamas to the legend of the contest

---

[7] *Hermes* 27 (1892) 378 n. 1.
[8] *Die Ilias und Homer* (1916) 396–439.

between the two poets is unclear and has been the subject of debate.⁹ It may be nothing more than the notion that Hesiod received the prize because he was the poet of peace whereas Homer was the poet of war. This would be in keeping with the humanitarian feelings of Alcidamas, who sympathized with the Messenians against the Spartans and declared that there is no natural distinction between free men and slaves.

Another subject which interested fifth-century readers was the life and thought of the Seven Wise Men. The so-called drinking songs of the Seven Wise Men quoted by Diogenes Laertius with the formula τῶν δὲ ᾀδομένων αὐτοῦ εὐδοκίμησε τάδε are generally recognized as fifth-century products. *Pap. Soc. It.* IX 1093, as Bruno Snell saw, virtually proves or confirms that a *Banquet of the Seven Wise Men* circulated in the fifth century B.C. In more popular quarters stories were told about the life of Aesop. Herodotus had some knowledge of it, as the curious anecdote in 2.134 about Aesop's murder in Delphi shows. It is more difficult to say whether details of the Delphic story of Aesop which we find in Plutarch, *De sera numinis vindicta* 12.557A (compare Plutarch *Solon* 28), go back to the fifth century.¹⁰

The legend of Archilochus, too, must have been in the process of developing in the fifth century, if not earlier. About 250 B.C. Mnesiepes referred in his inscription in the Archilocheion of Paros to ancient traditions about Archilochus. One of these traditions was the encounter of Archilochus with the Muses. To the best of our knowledge Archilochus never claimed to have met the Muses. The episode, obviously modelled on Hesiod, was invented by Archilochus' admirers. It has been suggested that this episode is represented on the Boston pyxis dating from about 450 B.C. If this is correct, it would confirm Mnesiepes' statement and place some elements

---

⁹ M. L. West, *Class. Quart.* 17 (1967) 433. Some of his points are controverted by V. Di Benedetto in a paper published in *Rend. Accad. Lincei* 1969. For further bibliography on Pap. Mich. 2754, cf. R. Pack, *The Greek and Latin Literary Texts from Greco-Roman Egypt* (1965²) p. 21 no. 76.

¹⁰ Snell, *Gesammelte Schriften* (1966) 115; La Penna, *Athenaeum* 40 (1969) 264.

of Archilochus' legend before 450 B.C.[11] One wonders how much of the biography of Sappho and Alcaeus—which interested both vase painters and Herodotus (2.135)—was put together in the fifth century.

If we knew more about the literary studies of Hellanicus, Damastes, and Glaucus of Rhegium, we should be in a better position to appreciate that research on the lives of the poets, of the Seven Wise Men, and even of the plebeian Aesop was part of the new urge to collect information about Greek literary antiquities. Hellanicus wrote an account of the winners of the Carnean games (καρνεονῖκαι) which included at least one excursus, if not more, on the development of music in Greece. Damastes wrote a work on poets and sophists, and Glaucus on "ancient poets and musicians." Hellanicus and Damastes, needless to say, were famous antiquarians. The title of Glaucus' book is clearly antiquarian.

The existence of real, full-fledged biographies of literary men is more doubtful. Theagenes may have written a biography of Homer. There is an increasing inclination among responsible scholars, such as F. Jacoby, to recognize in the substance of the so-called Herodotean life of Homer a fifth-century document—though not of course from Herodotus' pen.[12]

The conclusion is that we must distinguish between *contributions* to biography (such as the *Agon* between Homer and Hesiod or the *Banquet of the Seven Wise Men*) and *real*, full-fledged biographies (such as the alleged lives of Homer). Contributions to biography are certain. The existence of fifth-century biography of poets and Wise Men is conjectural, but, I should say, altogether likely.

II

If literary biography takes us among the sophists and other learned men of the late fifth century, political biography and

---

[11] *Archilochus,* ed. I. Tarditi (Rome 1968), with bibl.

[12] Wilamowitz, *Ilias und Homer,* 413–439; Jacoby, *Hermes* 68 (1933) 10 = *Kleine Philologische Schriften* I (1961) 11; R. Pfeiffer, *History of Classical Scholarship,* 11.

autobiographical travel books seem to have their origins in Ionia half a century earlier. We are told that Skylax of Caryanda—the man who explored the Indian coasts by order of Darius I and wrote a report on his journey (Herodotus 4.44; Aristotle *Politics* 7.13.2)—was also the man who wrote a life of Heraclides, the famous contemporary tyrant of Mylasa (Herodotus 5.121). This piece of information comes from a problematic entry in the *Suda* and has often been doubted, but without sufficient reason. The title given by the *Suda* is τὰ κατὰ Ἡρακλείδην τὸν Μυλασσῶν βασιλέα. This means: "The story of the tyrant (or king) Heraclides of Mylasa," just as τὰ κατὰ τὸν Τέλλον in Herodotus 1.31 means "The story of Tellus." Skylax of Caryanda was obviously the man to write about Heraclides of Mylasa.[13] Any other theory has to postulate the existence either of a different Skylax or of a different Heraclides—or even of a different Skylax writing about a different Heraclides—which is a waste of ingenuity. We do not know what Skylax' book was like and whether it was a complete biography of Heraclides. But it was a book telling the story of an individual. Skylax appears to have written some sort of biographical work in the decades about 480 B.C. Sosylus, the historian of Hannibal, may have directly or indirectly derived from Skylax his information about Heraclides' stratagem in a naval battle (*FGrHist* 176F1).

Skylax may also have written a work with autobiographical features. The account he gave of his geographical explorations was inevitably a kind of partial autobiography. Accounts of travels, whether written or oral (to begin with the *Odyssey*), must be regarded as predecessors of autobiography. Eduard Norden showed this long ago. What characterizes Skylax is that the account of his journey was written in prose and

---

[13] H. Bengtson, *Historia* 3 (1954) 303 must be revised by taking into account L. H. Jeffery, *Ann. Brit. School Athens* 57 (1962) 126. F. Jacoby, *FGrHist* 709T1 (1958) seems to agree with what I state in the text, but see his almost contemporary (1957) "Nachträge" (2nd ed.) to *FGrHist* 10 (p. 543) with their warning. Cf. also F. Gisinger, *RE* III A, 634f.

described real travel. There was more truth in his works than in the epic poems that went before them.

Next we know that in about 440 B.C. Ion of Chios wrote an account of travels—or rather, in his case, of visits (᾿Επιδημίαι) —in which he told of some of his personal adventures and encounters, such as the meeting with Pericles and Sophocles during the Samian War. There is no reason to believe that Ion told his own life from birth, but his tale was of a definite autobiographical character and a delight to read, to judge from the fragments.

Thirdly, we have fairly extensive fragments of the pamphlet written by Stesimbrotus of Thasus on Themistocles, Thucydides, son of Melesias, and Pericles. It used to be classified as an anti-Athenian pamphlet by an exile from Thasus, a victim of Pericles' policies. But Fritz Schachermeyr has shown that Stesimbrotus probably wrote his pamphlet some years after the death of Pericles.[14] The new date invites us to reconsider the purpose of the pamphlet. According to Schachermeyr, Stesimbrotus was a literary man who was more interested in recording the peculiarities of political leaders than in attacking their politics. He seems to have been the predecessor of the later writers of monographs on tyrants and demagogues. The name which immediately comes to mind for comparison is Theopompus, who devoted an excursus of his *Philippica* to the Athenian demagogues. Here again, if we have no full-fledged biography, we have an antecedent.

Finally, Diogenes Laertius in his life of Empedocles (8.63) gives a strange piece of information. He writes: "Aristotle too declares him [Empedocles] to have been a champion of freedom and averse to rule of every kind, seeing that, as Xanthus relates in his account of him, he declined the kingship when it was offered to him, obviously because he preferred a frugal life." This passage raises all sorts of problems. Diogenes Laertius gives a quotation of Xanthus within a quotation of Aristotle. We should like to know whether the

---

[14] *Sitzungsb. Oesterr. Akad.* 247, 5, 1965.

name of Xanthus was mentioned by Aristotle or was added by Diogenes Laertius or by an intermediate source. We should also like to be certain that the Xanthus here mentioned is Xanthus of Lydia, the historian contemporary with Herodotus. And, if Xanthus of Lydia is meant, we should like to be certain that his name was not used by a later forger or historical novelist to deceive his readers. Nor are we certain that in referring to an account of Empedocles Diogenes Laertius meant a biography. Yet I find it difficult to believe that Diogenes Laertius had in mind anybody but the famous Xanthus of Lydia. I also believe that his Greek implies that in his opinion Xanthus had written a book on Empedocles. What has been prudently translated as "Xanthus in his account of Empedocles" reads in Greek: καθάπερ Ξάνθος ἐν τοῖς περὶ αὐτοῦ λέγει. This is Diogenes Laertius' normal terminology indicating "a monograph about a certain man." For instance, καθὰ καὶ ᾽Απολλώνιος ὁ Τύριος ἐν τοῖς περὶ Ζήνωνός φησι (7.6): "Apollonius of Tyre says in his work about Zeno." Even if Diogenes Laertius did not mean that Xanthus had written a book on Empedocles, he at least implied that Xanthus had written at length on Empedocles.

I am much less certain that Aristotle quoted Xanthus and therefore vouches for the authenticity of the quotation. But Aristotle also knew that Empedocles left unfinished a poem on Xerxes' expedition to Greece (frag. 70 Rose = Diogenes Laertius 8.57)—a tantalising piece of information, for which Xanthus seems the obvious source.[15]

Neither the chronology of Empedocles' life nor that of Xanthus' has been established with sufficient certainty to allow us to say that Xanthus could not have written about Empedocles. Xanthus may have been active after 420 B.C. He may have had many good reasons for being interested in the Sicilian thinker: he was also interested in Zoroaster, according to a statement in Diogenes Laertius' preface (*FGrHist*

---

[15] J. Bidez and F. Cumont, *Les Mages Hellénisés* I (1938) 238–240. H. Herter, *RE* IX A, 1355f.

765F32) which A. D. Nock successfully defended against many doubts.[16]

All in all, I do not see anything inherently improbable in the attribution of a life of Empedocles to Xanthus of Lydia. The Asiatic origin of Xanthus is an argument in favour of the authenticity of the account of Empedocles attributed to him. We shall soon see that interest in biographical stories was more widespread in Asiatic than in metropolitan Hellas. Jacoby must have had the same impression, because he included the passage of Diogenes Laertius on Empedocles among the authentic fragments of Xanthus the Lydian (*FGrHist* 765F33). Here again we have to distinguish between contributions to biography or to autobiography which are certain (such as the works by Stesimbrotus and Ion) and full-fledged biographies which are merely probable in varying degrees of probability (such as those we have attributed to Skylax and Xanthus).

To sum up, the evidence is neither abundant nor beyond suspicion; but it allows us to say that both biographical and autobiographical works were known in the fifth century B.C. —even outside the narrow sphere of literary and mythological biography. A few of these works, such as the lives of Theseus and of Homer and perhaps those of Aesop and of Heraclides the tyrant of Mylasa, seem to have been biographies according to the definition of a biography as an account of a life from birth to death. Other works may simply have been accounts of specific episodes of the life of a man.

The value of the evidence I have collected lies, to my mind, mainly in the warning it contains. Too much of fifth-century Greek literature has been lost. Those who put the origins of biography in the fourth century B.C. forget this warning. They seem to assume that what is lost never existed.

The warning is necessary in a field which inevitably leads us to consider relations between Greeks and non-Greeks. Our information about the early fifth century is particularly deficient in the field of international cultural relations. I will

---

[16] *American Journal of Archaeology* 53 (1949) 275.

only recall two episodes because they are indirectly relevant to our search. In 1942, during the war, Professor Jacques Perret created a sensation in France with his thesis *Les origines de la légende troyenne de Rome*. He seemed to have proved that Pyrrhus, king of Epirus, invented the legend of the Trojan origin of the Romans in 280 B.C. Owing to the war Professor Perret did not know that while he was writing his thesis Professor Giglioli in Rome had published archaic statuettes of Aeneas shouldering Anchises which had been discovered at Veii. The exact date of these statuettes, which seem to belong to the early fifth century B.C., does not matter: what became evident was that the legend of Aeneas was familiar to Etruscans and Romans at least two centuries before Pyrrhus. The cult of Aeneas in Italy had nothing to do with him. A few years ago Professor Alföldi gave seven reasons for refusing to believe that Rome had made a pact with Carthage about 500 B.C.[17] While his book was in proof Professor Pallottino published the famous inscriptions of Pyrgi—two in Etruscan and one in Phoenician—which made it evident that Rome and Carthage could not ignore each other about 500 B.C., at a time when Rome's neighbour Caere was under heavy Phoenician influence.

Both Perret and Alföldi had underrated the existing literary evidence which contradicted their theories, but above all they had underrated the extent of our ignorance of the affairs of the Mediterranean world about 500 B.C. In each case one casual discovery was enough to refute a priori contentions of able scholars.

III

Let us now consider some of the names included in our previous discussion. Two names belong to Asia Minor, indeed to marginal zones of Greek culture: Skylax of Caryanda and Xanthus the Lydian. The other two writers, Ion of Chios and Stesimbrotus of Thasus, were islanders. This point is important if seen in conjunction with one of the most

[17] A. Alföldi, *Early Rome and the Latins* (1965) 350.

striking features of Greek historiography of the fifth century B.C. Though Herodotus was obviously very interested in the family of the Alcmaeonids, in Themistocles, Cleomenes, Leonidas, and so forth, what he has to say about the life of the most important Greek leaders is very little. He can tell long stories about Cyrus, Cambyses, and Croesus or about Greek men who served the Persian kings, such as the doctor Democedes and the elder Miltiades (6.34ff). In these cases, as Professor Homeyer has shown, he organized his material according to principles of formal biography: origins, youth, achievements, death. But evidently he found more biographical material in Asia Minor than in metropolitan Greece. Even the stories of Cypselus and of the Alcmaeonids, the most conspicuous to come from metropolitan Greece, did not amount to more than isolated episodes (5.92, 6.125). This conclusion seems to be supported by what we read in Thucydides. His disinclination to give biographical details is obvious. It may reflect aristocratic disdain for personal details: in Athens private circumstances were made public and exploited by writers of comedy and hostile orators or demagogues. But this cannot be the whole truth. Thucydides did in fact put right essential details of the lives of Harmodius, Themistocles, and Pausanias because nobody had taken the trouble to do so before.[18] Thucydides was interested in biography, but some invisible barrier seems to have prevented him from pursuing this interest in Athens. The very episodes of Themistocles and Pausanias about which he wrote belonged to the history of Greco-Persian relations and had happened outside metropolitan Greece. Thucydides may have collected information about them during his exile. This would bear out the lack of interest of contemporary Athenians in the lives of the great men of the preceding generation.

The impression one forms in reading Herodotus and Thucy-

[18] Cf. for instance H. Münch, *Studien zu den Exkursen des Thucydides* (Heidelberg 1935); F. Jacoby, *Atthis* (1949) 158; O. Lendle, *Hermes* 92 (1964) 129; A. Lippold, *RhM* 108 (1965) 336; C. W. Fornara, *Philologus* 111 (1967) 291 and *Historia* 17 (1968) 400.

dides is that interest in biographical details about political figures was more alive in Asia Minor and generally in Ionian culture than in Athens and other centres of metropolitan Greece during the fifth century B.C. Can this difference be explained in terms of cultural influences?

The question is at least worth asking. Interest in kings and tyrants is natural where kings and tyrants rule. When Greeks began to write historical prose, Ionia was being ruled by Persian kings and local tyrants. Furthermore, Asia Minor was exposed to Oriental tales with their strong biographical flavour. The stories about the Seven Wise Men may owe something to their oriental counterparts which go back to the Gilgamesh epos. These stories were apparently first recorded in Asia Minor. References to them begin with Hipponax. The meeting of the Seven Wise Men at Croesus' court is implied in Herodotus 1.29, though the first explicit reference is in Ephorus (*FGrHist* 70F181). According to Clement of Alexandria, *Stromata* 1.15.69, Democritus made his own (plagiarized?) the sayings of Aḥiqar. The Aramaic version of the story of Aḥiqar is known to have circulated among the Jews of Elephantina in the fifth century B.C. The reliability of Clement on this point is notoriously controversial: E. Meyer substantially accepted it;[19] H. Diels (*Vorsokratiker*[6] II.209) gave his reasons for rejecting it. What is certain in any case is that Theophrastus was acquainted with the story of Aḥiqar (Diogenes Laertius 5.50), which means that it must have made its way to Greece either in the fifth or in the fourth century B.C. It got mixed up rather soon with the story of Aesop, which reveals oriental influences in many other details. The essential data are collected in Professor B. E. Perry's introduction to his Loeb edition of Babrius and Phaedrus (1965). Autobiography was a well-cultivated literary genre in various countries of the Persian Empire from Egypt to Assyria.[20] Both Jews and Greeks reformed their political

---

[19] *Der Papyrusfund von Elephantine* (3rd ed. 1912) 123–125.

[20] The best description of the various types of oriental historiography is perhaps in E. Täubler, "Die Anfänge der Geschichtsschreibung" in *Tyche*

life and their culture and redefined their national identity in relation to the Persians. We may therefore wonder whether it is a matter of pure coincidence that in the fifth century Nehemiah and perhaps Ezra wrote autobiographies in Judaea, while Ion wrote his autobiographical memoirs in Chios. Nehemiah's autobiography was a novelty in Judaea just as much as Ion's autobiographical notes were a novelty in Greece.[21]

We are not looking for precise models for Greek biographies and autobiographies in the East. We cannot do so, because we have no clear idea of what Skylax and Xanthus put into their biographical work. But we cannot easily discount the impression that it is of historical significance that both Skylax and Xanthus, the first biographers in the Greek language known to us, were Persian subjects. Indeed Xanthus was no Greek at all.

Given our evidence, we are unable to visualize in what way Greeks and non-Greeks interchanged cultural goods in the fifth century B.C. But there are occasional glimpses. One is Herodotus' allusion to the Persian Zopyrus "who deserted from the Persians to Athens" (3.160) and who obviously told

---

(1926) 17–74; cf. also R. Laqueur, *Neue Jahrb. f. Wiss. und Jugendb.* 7 (1931) 489–506. On oriental autobiographical inscriptions, S. Mowinckel, "Die vorderasiatischen Königs- und Fürsteninschriften," *Eucharisterion H. Gunkel* (1923) 278–322, is fundamental. Cf. W. Baumgartner, *Orient. Literaturz.* (1924) 313–317; H. Gese, *Zeitschr. f. Theol. und Kirche* 55 (1958) 127–145. On Egypt, E. Otto, *Die biographischen Inschriften der ägyptischen Spätzeit* (1954). On Assyria cf. especially H.-G. Güterbock, *Zeitschr. f. Assyriologie* 8 (1934) 1–91 and 10 (1938) 45–149. In general E. A. Speiser in *The Idea of History in the Ancient Near East* (1955) 37–76. An important text is S. Smith, *The Statue of Idri-mi,* 1949. We need a more precise typology of oriental biographical and autobiographical texts.

[21] It will be enough to refer to G. von Rad, *Zeitschr. f. Alttest. Wiss.* 76 (1964) 176–187; S. Mowinckel, *Studien zu dem Buche Ezra-Nehemia* I–III, especially II, Oslo 1964–1965; U. Kellermann, *Nehemia: Quellen, Ueberlieferung und Geschichte* (1967) 56–87.

Earlier biographical elements in the Bible are discussed by J. Hempel, *Geschichten und Geschichte im Alten Testament bis zur persischen Zeit* (1964). On the special problems of the so-called Baruch biography in Jeremiah cf. for instance A. Weiser, *Glaube und Geschichte im Alten Testament* (1961) 321–329; O. Eissfeldt, *Einleitung in das Alte Testament* (3rd ed., 1964).

him the story of his grandfather at the siege of Babylon. Herodotus also shows awareness of oriental biographical inscriptions, though he could not read them (2.106; 4.87; 4.91). Skylax' report of his sea voyage can hardly be separated from Hanno's account of his journey, which belongs to the fifth century, and probably to its first half. Hanno's account of his travels seems to have been translated from Phoenician into Greek only in the fourth or third century B.C.[22] Other similar texts may have been translated earlier. The bilingual *res gestae* which Hannibal left behind in Italy are rooted in a tradition of autobiographical inscriptions in Carthage, which in its turn was connected with oriental models. Darius' Behistun inscription was certainly no model for Nehemiah, Ion, or Hanno; each of these texts reflects a different religious and political outlook. But just as the Jews of Elephantina had a copy of the Aramaic text of Darius' autobiography, so the Ionians must have had copies of its translation into Greek. Autobiography was in the air in the Persian Empire of the early fifth century, and both Jews and Greeks may have been stimulated by Persian and other oriental models to create something of their own. We must dismiss the old preconception that all the autobiographies of the East were religious documents and uniform. What has come down to us is varied enough; and at the same time what we have is no fair sample of what has been lost.

These are random remarks from which it would be foolish to draw any firm conclusion. Biographical research about literary and artistic personalities of the past developed in connection with specific philosophical and cultural interests of the Greeks and appears to have been an independent achievement. External influences, if any, would, however, have affected: (a) autobiographies; (b) anecdotes (entertaining

[22] Cf. for instance R. Sénac, "Le périple du Carthaginois Hannon," *Bull. Assoc. G. Budé* 4, 4 (1966) 510–538, for recent discussion, but S. Gsell, *Hist. ancienne de l'Afrique du Nord* (3rd ed. 1921) I 468–523, is still basic. Most accessible ed. of the text in C. Müller, *Geographi graeci minores* I (1855). Hannibal's bilingual *res gestae*: Livy 28.46.16.

stories) about Aesop, Wise Men, and international adventurers like Democedes; (c) biographies of contemporaries (such as the life of Heraclides by Skylax?; and the life of Empedocles by Xanthus?).

IV

It remains true that neither biography nor autobiography became prominent literary genres in Greece in the fifth century B.C. We cannot generalize about society in the fifth century. But at least for Athens we can say that the cultural background as a whole did not favour the prominence of biography or autobiography.

Neither tragedy nor sculpture, as practised in the fifth century, displayed skill in biographical techniques. The interest of the poets who wrote tragedy was in decisive situations—situations from which inescapable consequences or at least inescapable alternatives followed. The idea of telling the life story of Oedipus or of Antigone step by step from birth to death in order to elucidate their characters and their importance is just the opposite of the tragic attitude. Tragedy must be entirely present to the spectators. As Aristotle perceived, there would be no possibility of *katharsis* if the spectators had to identify themselves with events they had not experienced. The same communication of the essential—to be apprehended at one glance—is characteristic of much, if not all, classical sculpture. The struggle between the Lapiths and the Centaurs on the western pediment at Olympia or the cavalcade on the frieze of the Parthenon are not episodes of a biography.

As I have intimated before, I have no desire to deny that even in Greek sculpture one might find embryonic attempts at biographical narration. It is a nice point whether the twelve metopes at Olympia describing Heracles' twelve canonic labours were meant to be read as sections of a biographical account. One might perhaps also find some biographical intention in vase painting, but the definition and discussion of it would take us too far. If we were prepared to see biographical episodes in certain vase scenes of about 500 B.C.—for instance Croesus on his pyre in Myson's amphora—this still would not take us beyond that preliminary stage of biography which is the single anecdote.

Comedy and history raise more troublesome questions in their relations to biography. Comedy is different from tragedy in that it makes the spectators uncertain about their position as spectators. The game of allusions, the play with parody, the contemporary setting compel the spectator to remember details of ordinary life and of individuals with whom he is personally acquainted. There is abundant biographical and autobiographical material in the comedies of Aristophanes.[23] We know that Hellenistic biographers exploited it for their biographies of fifth-century Athenians. But by the time they did this, Aristophanes and his public had long been dead. Fifth-century comedy was meant to make people laugh at situations to which they could not feel extraneous: it was no objective contribution to the biography of Socrates or Cleon or Euripides.

The relation between history and biography is bound to come up in various contexts here. Greek historians were concerned with political and military events. Their subject matter was states, not individuals. The close connection between history and geography emphasized concern with the community rather than with the individual. Herodotus and Thucydides wrote in a period in which the most important decisions were taken by the states in their councils and assemblies. This produced or at least reinforced the impression that military and political transactions were in the hands of collective bodies. Other new sciences, such as medicine, confirmed this collective approach. Men living in different parts of the earth were ipso facto assumed to have different attitudes or

---

[23] Aristophanes talks directly about his past experiences in the parabasis of some of his comedies, notably in the *Knights, Clouds, Wasps,* and *Peace.* This form of autobiographical speech remained confined, as far as I know, to Old Comedy: see W. Kranz in *RE* XVIII, s.v. "Parabasis."

abilities. Stable connections were postulated between climates and constitutions, and in their turn constitutions were supposed to condition the behaviour of individuals. The intellectual atmosphere in which history was born was one of faith in collective organization and of trust in natural explanations. It was a reaction to the faith in individual salvation and to the admiration for individual exploits which had characterized the age of the tyrants. Orators were not allowed to mention individual names when they delivered the official funeral speech for the dead in war. All this, of course, affected Herodotus less than Thucydides, the history of the Persian Wars less than the history of the Peloponnesian Wars. But the trend is clear in Herodotus also. The Spartans and the Athenians, not Leonidas and Themistocles, are Herodotus' protagonists of the Persian Wars. There is no indispensable Achilles or Hector in them—which shows the limits of Herodotus' debt to Homer. The idea that one could treat the Persian or the Peloponnesian Wars in biographical terms never dawned upon the mind of any Greek historian of the fifth century.

No history, however bent on emphasizing collective decisions, can manage to get rid of the disturbing presence of individuals: they are simply there. Indeed the Greek historians never denied that individuals affected military and political events. The very practice of democracy implied trust in leaders and created the climate for schools for leaders—as the sophists' schools were. Military leadership was recognized as a specific ability. The Athenian strategoi were elected, not chosen by lot like judges and councillors. One can go a step further. The discovery of history as a new intellectual discipline implied the recognition that understanding of human affairs was both possible and valuable. In so far as the politician was committed to the understanding of political affairs, there was an obvious similarity between the politician and the historian. Thucydides at least had no doubt that his ability to understand human affairs was akin to that of Pericles. Education, mental alertness, specific competence, and seriousness were to him factors of success both in politics and in historical writing. I have sometimes suspected that Thucydides saw Herodotus as a Cleon among the historians. Both Cleon and Herodotus tried to please their readers: both were demagogues, in Thucydides' eyes. But Thucydides confined his appreciation of individuals to their contribution to political life in specific moments: and so after all did Herodotus in the case of most Greek politicians. The value of the individual lay in his contribution to the welfare of the state to which he belonged. That excluded biography.

Historiography took the Greeks by surprise in the fifth century. It was the creation of a few men—Hecataeus, Herodotus, Thucydides, Hellanicus. There was very little preparation for it in the preceding century. The powerful personalities of the first historians imposed history on a public which was much more interested in tragedy, comedy, oratory, sophistic discussions. History remained what the first historians made it: a study of political and military actions. There was no desire to probe deeply into its foundations, to re-examine the role of the individuals in it. Indeed the implicit separation between biography and history of the fifth and fourth centuries B.C. was to become explicit later, at least from Polybius onwards.

One word more before I take leave of the fifth century B.C. I have tried to give what evidence I think exists for biography in the fifth century, but I have not tried to speculate on the awakening of the Greek biographical spirit. I deeply respect recent works on *La naissance de l'histoire* (which is the title of a book by François Chatelet) or on *The Awakening of the Greek Historical Spirit* (which is the title of a book by Professor Chester Starr). Personally, however, I suspect that this search for what made historiography or biography possible in the fifth century B.C. is bound to be vague and not very rewarding. Professor Starr, for instance, finds the conditions for the awakening of the Greek historical spirit in the world of the epic, in the colonial expansion of the Greeks, in a new awareness of time, in the rise of the polis, in the new individualism of lyric poetry. All these phenomena—and one could add many others, such as the monologues of heroes in epic poetry—have some vague connection with the creation of historiography and biography, but they belong to earlier centuries. They are neither contemporary with the rise of historiography and biography nor with each other. Either taken one by one or taken together, they do not explain the appearance of the first historical and biographical books in the fifth century.

For those who care to understand the mood which characterizes the little we know of biographical research in the fifth century, the extant fragments of Ion and Stesimbrotus are better guides. We can observe curiosity for the ways of eminent men, taste for the adroit answer, dislike for political opponents. With more diffidence and reserve, and therefore with fewer personal dislikes, the same mood is to be found in Herodotus.

III   The Fourth Century

I

As soon as we turn to the fourth century the change is obvious. We no longer have to explore remote corners to find evidence of interest in biography and autobiography. We no longer have to ask why the contemporaries of great Greek men were so little interested in them. The evidence for interest in biography and autobiography becomes abundant and permeates all aspects of literature. Funerary monuments confirm this interest by their presentation of intimate personal and family life. I shall only recall the well-known fact that in the fourth century B.C. epigrams on tombs contain more biographical details than those of former centuries. Age, place of birth, name of father, cause of death become more frequent elements of an epitaph. Thus Asclepiades Maeander is presented as a successful doctor who followed the profession of his father Maeander.[1] In the joint monument of Philagros of Angele and Hegilla daughter of Philagros, the daughter gives her age and says that her husband will bear witness to her virtues (Peek 107). In an epigram from Thebes young Timocles, son of Asopichos, has his victories in the horse races exactly recorded (Peek 95). Visitors to sanctuaries recorded their experiences on stone. More particularly the patients in the sanctuaries of Asclepius were talkative about

[1] W. Peek, *Griech. Grabgedichte* (1962) no. 82.

their experiences. This later developed into the autobiographical effusions of Aelius Aristides.[2]

On the other hand, the attempts at biography and autobiography in the first part of the fourth century do not seem to be a direct continuation of the analogous attempts of the fifth century. I speak here with great hesitation because we have seen how little is known about biography and autobiography in the fifth century. But three or four facts seem to have emerged from our search. In the fifth century there was at least one attempt to write the life of a man: this was the biography of Heraclides of Mylasa by Skylax. The same Skylax produced some sort of autobiographical account in his book on his travels. Ion of Chios also wrote a book of personal recollections in his 'Επιδημίαι. There was a great deal of research into the biography of poets of the past; and it is possible that Xanthus of Lydia gave a biographical sketch of Empedocles. Now we do not know of anything of this kind for the first half of the fourth century. One possible explanation of such discontinuities is that we are the victims of our imperfect information. It is possible that there never were any biographies of Heraclides and of Empedocles in the fifth century and that we have been misled by our sources; alternatively, it is possible that our sources are silent about similar attempts of the early fourth century which constituted the link between fifth-century and late fourth-century biography and autobiography. But our evidence, as far as it goes, really points to a different conclusion: namely that the fifth-century experiments in biography came to a sudden end and that in the fourth century biography and autobiography made a fresh start. The situation is not without analogies in

[2] The inscriptions of the sanctuary of Asclepius in Epidaurus are, however, not autobiographical accounts, but a semi-official registration of miracles. For such books of 'Επιφάνειαι see R. Herzog, *Die Wunderheilungen von Epidauros* (1931) 49. But even in the fourth century B.C. there were registrations of miracles in the first person. See for instance Aeschines' epigram, *Anth. Pal.* 6.330 (Herzog, p. 39) and Isyllus' poem E, where the first and third persons alternate (U. v. Wilamowitz-Moellendorff, *Isyllos von Epidauros* [1886] 22–29; *IG* IV², 128.57–79).

other cultures. In England Cavendish's life of Wolsey and Roper's life of More represented the foundations of a new tradition of biography. But the subsequent Elizabethan Age was poor in memorable biographies. Francis Bacon complained: "I do find it strange . . . that the writing of lives should be no more frequent." The details will emerge from our survey of the biographical and autobiographical explorations of the fourth century before Alexander the Great. But some of the general features of the new situation can easily be indicated beforehand and related to the new political, social, and intellectual climate.

In the fourth century individual politicians found themselves in a position of power very different from that of their predecessors in the previous century. In the fifth century Miltiades, Themistocles, Leonidas, even Pericles and Cleon, had been the servants of the state to which they belonged. The tyrants of Sicily had been the exception, which disappeared in the course of the century. In the fourth century the initiative passes to states which built up their new power under the guidance of individual leaders. The conservative states, such as Sparta and Athens, have to adapt themselves to the new situation. Hence the new power of professional military commanders; hence ultimately the emergence of a professional politician like Demosthenes who cannot rely on the steady support of his city as Pericles had done, but has to establish or re-establish his authority in a succession of crises within his own city. In the fourth century Lysander, Conon, Agesilaus, Dionysius the Elder, Epaminondas, Philip of Macedon, and ultimately Demosthenes and Alexander the Great have a personal political line. They represent, as individuals, a greater source of hope and fear than the Athenian and Spartan politicians of the fifth century.

The new trends in philosophy and rhetoric emphasized the importance of individual education, performance, self-control. We have denied that the origins of biography are to be exclusively connected with Socrates and the Socratics. We have tried to show that the most ancient evidence for Greek biographical and autobiographical work is earlier than Socrates. This has thrown doubt also on F. Leo's thesis that Hellenistic biography is a product of the Aristotelian school and therefore in some sense a Socratic product. But this does not mean denying the obvious—namely that the Socratics were the leaders in biographical experiments in the fourth century.

II

The Socratics were infuriating in their own time. They are still infuriating in our time. They are never so infuriating as when approached from the point of view of biography. We like biography to be true or false, honest or dishonest. Who can use such terminology for Plato's *Phaedo* or *Apology*, or even for Xenophon's *Memorabilia*? We should all like to dismiss Plato, who cared too much about the bigger truth to be concerned with the smaller factual accuracy. We should like to save Xenophon the honest mediocre historian, who told the facts as he knew them best, by damning Xenophon the Socratic memorialist, who lost interest in historical correctness. But the fact we have to face is that biography acquired a new meaning when the Socratics moved to that zone between truth and fiction which is so bewildering to the professional historian. We shall not understand what biography was in the fourth century if we do not recognize that it came to occupy an ambiguous position between fact and imagination. Let us be in no doubt. With a man like Plato, and even with a smaller but by no means simpler man like Xenophon, this is a consciously chosen ambiguity. The Socratics experimented in biography, and the experiments were directed towards capturing the potentialities rather than the realities of individual lives. Socrates, the main subject of their considerations (there were other subjects, such as Cyrus), was not so much the real Socrates as the potential Socrates. He was not a dead man whose life could be recounted. He was the guide to territories as yet unexplored. Remember Phaedo's words: "I thought that in going to the other world he could

not be without a divine call, and that he would be happy, if
any man ever was, when he arrived there; and therefore I did
not pity him as might have seemed natural at such an hour"
(transl. B. Jowett). In Socratic biography we meet for the
first time that conflict between the superior and the inferior
truth which has remained a major problem for the student of
the Gospels or of the lives of Saints. Nor is this the only type
of ambiguity we discover in fourth-century biography. If
philosophy introduced the search for the soul, rhetoric introduced the search for the improving word: anything can
appear better or more than it is, if the right word is used.
Plato sensed his enemy in Isocrates and the enmity was
cordially reciprocated.

The fourth century is a time of strong, self-willed personalities which offer plenty of good opportunities to biographers.
But it is also a time of divergent and conflicting explorations
of the limits of human life, in terms of philosophy or in terms
of rhetoric.

Both Plato and Xenophon apparently created new types of
biographical and autobiographical narration: Xenophon
especially must be regarded as a pioneer experimenter in
biographical forms. Behind them there is the problematic
personality of Antisthenes—an older man who, if we knew
him better, might easily appear an original and powerful
contributor to biography. Apart from writing two dialogues
on Cyrus, which may have influenced Xenophon's *Cyropaedia,* Antisthenes composed a book (perhaps a dialogue) on
Alcibiades. This book certainly discussed details of Alcibiades' life, especially his relation to Socrates. It is going too
far to describe it as a biography of Alcibiades, as Mullach did
in the *Fragmenta Philosophorum Graecorum*; but it contributed
to Alcibiades' biography. Antisthenes also wrote an attack
against Athenian politicians in general, which was inevitably
full of biographical details.[3] Nor must we forget that Theo-

---

[3] See *Antisthenis Fragmenta,* collegit F. Decleva Caizzi (1966), for texts and
bibliography.

pompus, the first historian to give a large place to biography, was an admirer of Antisthenes, whose skill he praised and whom he declared capable of winning over whomever he wanted by means of agreeable discourse (Diogenes Laertius 6.14).

Yet Theopompus was also, and even more, a pupil of Isocrates; and Isocrates has his part in the history of biography. In his turn Isocrates cannot be separated from the general trends of rhetorical and forensic eloquence which contributed more than is usually admitted to the technique of biographical and autobiographical accounts. I hope I am not surprising anyone if I say that I shall later treat Demosthenes' *De corona* as an autobiographical document. The technique for winning lawsuits and making political propaganda relied generally on the ability to present one's own and somebody else's life in a suitable light. The earliest extant biography of Alcibiades is in the speech Isocrates wrote for Alcibiades' son about 397 B.C.: the speech "On the Team of Horses." Later Isocrates added something of his own. He proposed a system of education which selected pupils according to inborn qualities and trained them according to a precise ideal of intellectual and moral perfection. He made it clear that eloquence was in itself productive of moral excellence. He also claimed for eloquence the old prerogative of poetry, which was to confer immortality by discovering and praising virtue. He defended this ideal in an autobiographical speech, "About the Exchange."

Isocrates' περὶ ἀντιδόσεως was never uttered before a court of law: it was a rhetorical exercise. But neither were the speeches which Plato and Xenophon put into the mouth of Socrates in self-defense ever uttered, at least not in that form. A conventional form of eloquence was used for new experiments. Being conventional, it set certain clear limits to the experiments. The biographic and autobiographic experiments of the fourth century see a man in relation to his profession, to his political community, to his school: they are portraits of public figures, not of private lives. The transitional character of these compositions is undeniable. The

picture becomes even more complex if we remember that
Isocrates was conscious of turning into prose that art of
encomium for which Pindar had been richly paid (see *Antidosis* 166). Xenophon, on the other hand, must have had the
portraits by Euripides, *Suppliants* (860ff), in his mind when he
wrote the portraits of the dead generals in the *Anabasis*. The
interplay between new political and social ideals and old
forms is an essential feature of fourth-century writing. At the
same time the search for rules of life had to reckon with the
new power of words. Plato's fear of being overpowered by
rhetoric is as real as Isocrates' fear of having his words
controlled by philosophers.

III

Isocrates' *Euagoras* was written about 370 B.C. Isocrates
was not new to biographical sketches in speeches. I have
already referred to the portrait of Alcibiades he drew in the
speech "On the Team of Horses" about 397 B.C. But the
Euagoras was something more ambitious. He considered it
to be the first attempt at a prose encomium by a contemporary.
Aristotle apparently did not accept this claim. In the first book
of his *Rhetorics* (1368a17) he implicitly claimed priority for an
obscure encomium for the Thessalian Hippolochus who, as
Wilamowitz said in one of his most temperamental *Lese-
früchte*,[4] was the boy for whom the courtesan Lais lost her life
at the beginning of the fourth century (Plutarch *Amatorius*
21.767F). But Isocrates may not have been conversant with
this Thessalian product. Isocrates described Euagoras as an
enquiring mind, a man who never thought of injustice and
gained friends by generosity. The encomium is organized in
chronological order but cannot properly be described as a
biography of Euagoras from birth to death. While the reac-
tions of Conon, of the king of Persia, and of the Spartans to
Euagoras' achievements are told at some length, there is
hardly one episode of Euagoras' life that can be said to be

---

4 *Hermes* 35 (1900) 533 = *Kl. Schriften* IV 111.

narrated. Isocrates combines rather ineffectually a static description of Euagoras' character with a chronological account
of what other people did to Euagoras.

A few years later, about 360, Xenophon took *Euagoras* as a
model for his *Agesilaus*. He had known Agesilaus personally;
he had written or was going to write about him in his Hel-
lenic History: the relation between the encomium of Agesilaus and the relevant sections of the *Hellenica* is notoriously a
matter of dispute. The very fact that he wrote twice on Agesilaus shows that he made a distinction between the historical
account of the *Hellenica* and the encomiastic (I do not say biographical) account of the pamphlet. He described the latter as
an ἔπαινος and an encomium, namely an appreciation of the
virtues and glory of the dead king. He therefore did for
Agesilaus what Isocrates had done for the dead Euagoras.
Like Isocrates before him, he must have been conscious of
turning into prose the traditional poetic eulogy of a dead
man; and he must also have shared Isocrates' belief or illusion
that there was no clear link between his·encomium and the
prose funeral speeches for dead men of earlier times.

Xenophon, however, was not the man to follow Isocrates
blindly. To begin with, he was much more interested in
Agesilaus' actual achievements than Isocrates had been in
Euagoras' deeds. He also had greater historical sense and
experience than Isocrates. He knew, for instance, that notable
sayings were normally not considered worth presenting in a
book of history (*Hellenica* 2.3.56). We shall later see that he
may have experimented with character drawing in the
Anabasis. The untidy mixture of static eulogy and chronological account was not easily acceptable to the historian of the
Anabasis and of the *Hellenica*. He therefore divided the encomium of Agesilaus into two parts. The first was written in
the chronological order suggested by Isocrates, but was more
factual. We can even say that it was much nearer to what later
became a conventional biography. The second part was a
nonchronological, systematic review of Agesilaus' virtues.
As Xenophon explains at the beginning of chapter 3, after

having given the record of the king's deeds he is now attempting to show the virtue that was in his soul. In arranging the praise of Agesilaus' virtues—"piety, justice, self-control, courage, wisdom, patriotism, urbanity"—he follows a scheme going back to Gorgias and adopted by other Socratics. There were also contingent reasons for such a systematic review of Greek virtues as typified by Agesilaus. Around 360 B.C. Xenophon was anxious to give an anti-Persian slant to his characterization of the Greek king: "I will next say how his behaviour contrasted with the *alazoneia*—the vain-boasting—of the Persian king." But the dichotomy between the chronological survey of events and the systematic analysis of inherent qualities was an attempt to solve one of the most difficult problems facing a biographer: how to define a character without sacrificing the variety of events of an individual life. When we talk of *Life and Works* or of *The Man and his Work* we are still within the borders of Xenophon's dichotomy.

The same Xenophon wrote character sketches of contemporaries in his *Anabasis*. This work was certainly composed before the *Agesilaus,* but its relation to the *Euagoras* is much more difficult to define. The portraits of Proxenus and Meno appear to be written in the antithetic style dear to Isocrates (*Anabasis* 2.6.16–29), whereas the other two portraits of Cyrus (1.9) and of Clearchus (2.6.1–15) are stylistically independent. Ivo Bruns, who called attention to this difference,[5] suggested that Xenophon had just written the portrait of Clearchus when Isocrates' *Euagoras* came into his hands: he hastened to imitate Isocrates in the portraits of Proxenus and Meno which follow that of Clearchus. This is too good to be true. It would of course imply a date for the *Anabasis* later than the publication of the *Euagoras*—that is, a terminus post quem of about 370 B.C. But even apart from the fact that there are more solid arguments for believing the contrary—namely that Isocrates had read the *Anabasis* when he published the *Panegyricus* in 380 B.C. (*Anabasis* 2.4.4 ∼ *Panegyricus*

---

[5] *Literar. Portr.,* 137ff.

149)—I am not convinced that the influence of Isocrates' *Euagoras* on the *Anabasis* exists. These portraits are not *encomia*. If anything, the portrait of Meno is a ψόγος, a censure. Taken together, the four portraits represent four different types of men. Cyrus is more complex: a loyal friend and a ruthless enemy, brave in war, skilful in administration. His chief quality is loyalty and generosity towards friends. The typological interest is directly emphasized in the case of Clearchus: "Now such a conduct as this, in my opinion, reveals a man fond of war." Proxenus is the ambitious man in a good sense, Meno in the bad sense. It is worth noticing that even in the brief portrait of Cyrus great importance is attributed to his education. There is here a clear indication of the interest which Xenophon was to develop later in writing about the education of the other Cyrus, *Cyropaedia*. My tentative conclusion is that Xenophon had already shown an independent inclination to draw character before he came across Isocrates' *Euagoras*. The portraits of the *Anabasis* are Xenophon's own, and the influence of Isocrates on the *Agesilaus* is secondary.

Xenophon made a third experiment in biographical writing with his *Apomnemoneumata*. We call them *Memorabilia,* the arbitrary title given to them by Johannes Leonclavius in 1569. The correct translation of *Apomnemoneumata* is *Commentarii*, which is the title given to Xenophon's work by Aulus Gellius (14.3): "libros quos dictorum atque factorum Socratis commentarios composuit." The unity of the work, which was disputed in the past, is now hardly in doubt. H. Erbse made it clear that the whole work, not only the first two chapters of the first book, is a defense of Socrates in a legal style, which has its parallels in Lysias 16.[6] Xenophon probably had in mind not the real accusers of Socrates, but the sophist Polycrates, who in about 393 B.C. had attacked Socrates' memory.[7]

[6] *Hermes* 89 (1961) 257.

[7] J. Humbert, *Polycratès, L'accusation de Socrate et le Gorgias* (1930); P. Treves, *RE* XXI 1736–1752; E. Gebhardt, *Polykrates' Anklage gegen Sokrates* (diss. Frankfurt 1957).

Polycrates had produced an imaginary judicial speech against Socrates, and Xenophon answers in a judicially acceptable form. After having concluded the defense in the first two chapters of book 1, he says at the beginning of chapter 3: "I propose to show how Socrates helped his companions both by his deeds and his words, and in order to do so, I shall relate all that I remember about them." This corresponds to the rule enunciated by Lysias: "In the *dokimasiai* one is justified in giving an account of the whole life." But in taking advantage of a legal device, Xenophon exploits it to an extent which makes it impossible to call his work an apology for Socrates. The report, the *Memorabilia* or *Commentarii*, became far more important than the apology.

Two questions interest us: whether Xenophon created the new literary genre of the *Memorabilia* and whether he intended to preserve real conversations of Socrates for posterity. We do not know of any *Memorabilia* before Xenophon. The fact that they combine a defense of Socrates with recollections of Socrates seems to speak for their originality.

Collections of sayings of philosophers and wise men had undoubtedly circulated in the fifth century. As we have seen, sayings of the Seven Wise Men were known before Socrates. Herodotus quotes some of them and knows that there were variants in the tradition (1.27). The popular wisdom of Aesop was known in the fifth century (Herodotus 2.134; Aristophanes *Wasps* 1446). It is also possible that written collections of Pythagorean sayings existed before Aristoxenus.[8] But a collection of philosophical conversations as given by Xenophon is another matter, for which I cannot quote an exact parallel in Greece. What we can say is that Xenophon became a model for later compilations. Zeno collected *Memorabilia* of Crates (Diogenes Laertius 7.4). Persaeus similarly tried to preserve recollections of Zeno and Stilpo in convivial dialogues which were apparently also called *Memorabilia* (Athenaeus

[8] On this complex question it will be enough to refer to C. J. De Vogel, *Pythagoras and Early Pythagoreanism* (1966).

4.162). This tradition has given us Epictetus' speeches, *Memorabilia*, or, as Stobaeus called them, *Apomnemoneumata Epictetou* (*Florilegium* 6.58–60, 29.84).

It is even more difficult to decide whether Xenophon intended to present real speeches. The question of Xenophon's intention is of course different from the question of whether Xenophon, even if he had intended to give the substance of real conversations in which Socrates had a leading part, was in a condition to fulfil his intention. The more one looks at the speeches, the less one can believe that Xenophon really intended to preserve the memory of the real Socrates. We may stretch our belief to accept that Socrates was waiting for the arrival of Xenophon to lecture his own son Lamprocles on his duties towards his mother (2.2). But the conversation between Socrates and Pericles the Younger is placed in the year in which the latter was a strategos (407 B.C.), though it reflects the situation of the Theban hegemony about 370 B.C. (3.5). The best research from K. Joël to O. Gigon has shown that what Xenophon does is to discuss topics which had been the subject of debate by other Socratics before him.[9] If Xenophon was not exactly the cynic Joël envisaged in his classic book, he learned perhaps more from Antisthenes' writings than from Socrates by word of mouth. All the Socratics were involved in elaborate developments of Socrates' thought which bore little resemblance to the original. The paradoxical conclusion from our point of view is that in the so-called *Memorabilia* Xenophon created or perfected a biographical form—the report of conversations preceded by a general introduction to the character of the main speaker—but in actual fact used this form for what amounted to fiction.

This brings us to a point which becomes even more evident in Xenophon's greatest contribution to biography, the

---

[9] K. Joël, *Der echte und der Xenophontische Sokrates*, 3 vols. (1893–1901); O. Gigon, *Sokrates: Sein Bild in Dichtung und Geschichte* (1947); J. Luccioni, *Xénophon et le Socratisme* (1953); A. H. Chroust, *Socrates: Man and Myth* (1957), where other bibl. Cf. E. Salin, *Platon und die griechische Utopie* (1921).

Cyropaedia. The *Cyropaedia* is indeed the most accomplished biography we have in classical Greek literature. It is a presentation of the life of a man from beginning to end and gives pride of place to his education and moral character. Nevertheless it is a paedagogical novel. The *Cyropaedia* was not, and probably never claimed to be, a true account of the life of a real person. Like Ctesias before him, Xenophon took advantage of his oriental subject to disregard historical truth. He was not the first of the Socratics to do so, if we may assume that Antisthenes' *Cyrus* preceded Xenophon's *Cyropaedia* in the same direction. The existence of previous Socratic writings of the same type may explain why Xenophon felt no need to warn his readers about the fictitious character of his biography: this was understood. But we shall never be able to tell exactly—even less than in the cases of Ctesias and Theopompus—how much is conscious fabrication of details and how much is elaboration of a tradition already rich in fictional elements. Xenophon had personal knowledge of the Persian state and of Persian institutions, and especially of the Persian army. He had Greek sources to supplement his information. He obviously tried to look plausible and well-informed. The last chapter of the *Cyropaedia* shows that he was concerned with the decline of the power of Persia just as in the *Constitution of Sparta* he had shown his concern for the decline of Sparta.

The papyri have definitely shown that erotic oriental romances existed in the first century after Christ, the date of the three extant fragments of the Ninus romance. The Ninus romance itself must be earlier than the date of the earliest papyri and goes back to 100 B.C. at least. We have therefore good reason to believe in the existence of a Hellenistic novel of oriental character. What interests us is that it claimed Xenophon's *Cyropaedia* as its model. It was remarked long ago that the *Suda* lexicon knows three Xenophons as authors of erotic romances, of which the alleged author of the extant story *Habrocomas and Anthia* is one. It seems probable that the name Xenophon in all these cases is a pseudonym or *nom de*

plume, which shows the popularity of the writer of the
Cyropaedia among writers and readers of novels. The
Cyropaedia included the episode of Abradatas and Panthea,
the classic example of a love story. Xenophon himself would
have been surprised to know that he had become the great
master and model of erotic stories: his *Cyropaedia* was highly
moral. But this was the price he had to pay for producing the
first biography, which was no biography at all, being a mixture of facts and fancies to communicate a philosophic
message.[10]

The *Cyropaedia* confirms a suspicion which the *Memorabilia*
had already suggested: namely that true biography was preceded or at least inspiringly accompanied by fiction. The suspicion is reinforced when we think of Herodotus and even
more of Ctesias. If Herodotus had honestly tried to separate
what he could vouch for from what he could not, Ctesias had
none of these preoccupations. He represented an uneasy
compromise between history and historical novel which
influenced Xenophon.[11] We might easily extend this consideration to Theopompus, who included in the *Philippica* a
long excursus on θαυμάσια, on wondrous happenings, which
gave a great deal of novelistic detail about religious prophets
—Zoroaster, Epimenides, Silenus, Bakis. Theopompus was
resolved to outbid Ctesias and perhaps Xenophon.[12]

This point is important for the understanding of ancient
biography at large even after the fourth century B.C. The
borderline between fiction and reality was thinner in biography than in ordinary historiography. What readers expected in biography was probably different from what they
expected in political history. They wanted information about
the education, the love affairs, and the character of their

[10] E. Rohde, *Der griechische Roman* (2nd ed. 1900) 372 n. 2; B. E. Perry, *The Ancient Romances,* (1967) 168. On Xenophon and the novel see also E. Schwartz, *Fünf Vorträge über den griechischen Roman* (reprint 1943); L. Giangrande, *Eranos* 60 (1962) 132–159.

[11] Bibl. in my essay on Ctesias, *Quarto Contributo* (1969) 181–212.

[12] Bibl. in W. R. Connor, *Theopompus and Fifth-Century Athens* (1968).

heroes. But these things are less easily documented than wars and political reforms. If biographers wanted to keep their public, they had to resort to fiction. Socratic philosophy and Isocratean rhetoric joined hands in encouraging the introduction of fiction into biography.

I purposely refrain from probing into this matter more deeply, and turn from biography to autobiography.

IV

The first name we meet in connection with fourth-century autobiography is again that of Xenophon. His *Anabasis* is for us the prototype of commentaries on a campaign written by one of the leading generals. He may have been preceded by his colleague Sophaenetus of Stymphalus, whose *Anabasis* is quoted by Stephanus Byzantius: but our ignorance of Sophaenetus is complete. E. Schwartz and F. Jacoby think of Sophaenetus' *Anabasis* as possibly a later forgery.[13] A satisfactory analysis of Xenophon's work in historiographical terms does not appear to exist. His *Anabasis* is under the influence of fifth-century travel literature in its geographical sections: we have seen that travel literature inevitably had an autobiographical character. In the matter of military campaigns Xenophon has learned something from Thucydides and perhaps also from Ctesias. But he describes military campaigns with a strongly subjective approach and a clearly apologetic tone: he had his enemies. To redress the balance he writes in the third person.[14] He apparently also uses the device of attributing his book to a non-existent Themistogenes. The *Anabasis* became a model both for its autobiographical character and for the effort to disguise it. The memorialistic literature of later times, to begin with

[13] E. Schwartz in A. von Mess, *RhM* 61 (1906) 372 n. 3; F. Jacoby, *FGrHist* 108–109, vol. II D, p. 349. Bux in *RE* III A 1008–1013 is unconvincing.

[14] The admirable excursus by E. Norden, *Agnostos Theos* (1923, reprint 1956) 313–331, on the first and third persons in historical accounts has not been replaced. A new comprehensive survey of the texts would be desirable.

Caesar, owes much to this double, partly contradictory, approach.

A very different kind of autobiographical production is the apologetic speech before a court of law. The famous model was the speech by Antiphon which Thucydides admired so much. It is all lost but for a fragment in a Geneva papyrus. What an authentic apology of this kind could be like is shown by Demosthenes' *De corona*, admittedly a later development of this genre: it was produced eighty years after Antiphon's speech in 330 B.C. Demosthenes chose the occasion for a complete apology for his anti-Macedonian policy. Part of the speech is inevitably nothing more than a personal attack by Demosthenes on his rival and accuser Aeschines. The rest is an attempt to make the audience realize under what conditions he, Demosthenes, had acted. Demosthenes never allows himself or his audience to forget that they have been defeated. But by placing his decisions in the proper context, he presents them as the only ones compatible with the honour of Athens and of himself. As he explains, it was inconceivable that Athens "should sink to such cowardice as by a spontaneous, voluntary act to surrender her liberty to Philip . . . The only remaining and the necessary policy was to resist with justice all his unjust designs" (69). Thus Demosthenes provides fragments of his autobiography against the background of the Athenian resistance to Macedon. He searches his own past. He has to defend himself and therefore the results of his search are predetermined. Yet one feels that his question—whether an alternative conduct was morally possible—is not a rhetorical one. The fascination of the *De corona* lies in its basic sincerity. The speech is autobiographical not only because it deals with episodes of Demosthenes' life but because it is unified by a strange, powerful, tantalizing examination of the whole of his past.

The real apologetic speech was bound to produce the artificial apology, the speech written not for a trial but for home reading in defense either of somebody else or of oneself. Neither Plato's nor Xenophon's Apologies of Socrates were ever uttered. Though presented as having been composed and pronounced by Socrates, they were in fact written by his pupils long after Socrates' death. They are biographical sketches disguised as autobiographical sketches. They show Socrates aware of what either Plato or Xenophon knew. We shall never know the exact relation of these two documents to Socrates' true speeches. Of course Plato's picture does not agree with that of Xenophon and is incomparably more profound; but both pictures have their limits fixed by the true terms of the indictment against Socrates. The fiction is anchored to truth: the pseudo-autobiography must be true biography to a certain extent.

Isocrates had Plato's pseudo-autobiography of Socrates in mind when he wrote his speech "About the Exchange" (περὶ ἀντιδόσεως, *Antidosis*) in about 354 B.C. But as an apologetic autobiography it is nevertheless authentic enough. Isocrates recounts his career as an educator and defends himself. Plato's *Apology*, a fictional speech and fictional autobiography of Socrates, is therefore the model for Isocrates' fictional speech, though the latter is authentic autobiography.

Isocrates' desire to play the part of Socrates in the fictional trial for which he wrote "About the Exchange" is indisputable. He thinks or imagines that, like Socrates, he has been accused of having corrupted Athenian youth by his educational methods: the accusation of tax evasion, for which he had really been impeached some time before, had only been a pretext. The ludicrous side of Isocrates' playing Socrates is so obvious that it is unnecessary to dwell on it. Isocrates was by now a very old man, and his sense of humour had not improved with the years. But he was still capable of new things, and what he did in this speech was new. He presented his life as an educator and as a writer of political speeches in an original way. He inserted an anthology of his other speeches into this speech. Furthermore, he was able to connect his educational activity very closely with Athenian politics in a way that no Socratic could have done, because Socrates had been prevented by his *daemon* from taking an active part in

Athenian politics. The speech as an apology for one's own literary activity within the context of public life was to inspire later autobiographical self-defenses. Libanius' so-called autobiography is the best known direct imitation of Isocrates' "About the Exchange,"[15] but Isocrates was in Cicero's mind when he wrote his *Brutus*.

The Socratics produced not only famous apologetic speeches which amounted to biography, though purporting to be autobiography: they also produced apologetic letters. The question we have to ask immediately is whether Plato's *Letter 7*, the greatest autobiographical letter of antiquity, is a real autobiography or a biographical letter disguised as autobiographical. Did a pupil of Plato write Plato's *Letter 7* just as Plato wrote Socrates' *Apology*? The question, needless to say, has been discussed ad nauseam. The latest study by Ludwig Edelstein is the most powerful plea I know of for the nonauthenticity of the letter.[16] The theory of nonauthenticity does not make an essential difference to the date of composition. Edelstein dates what he takes to be a forgery between 345 and 335 B.C., which represents a maximum of twenty years later than the date we would assign to the letter if it were authentic. The real question is the one I have mentioned: whether the letter is true autobiography or biography disguised as autobiography.

Two arguments make me inclined to take the letter as authentic, though I realize that, in strict logic, they are not decisive. The first argument is that Plato had authentic models for his fictional *Apology* of Socrates, but we do not

[15] On Isocrates, H. Peter, *Wahrheit und Kunst: Geschichtschreibung und Plagiat im Klassischen Altertum* (1911) 144–151 is worth remembering: the whole book is relevant. On Libanius, A. F. Norman, *Libanius' Autobiography (Oration I)*, 1965; cf. also the German translation with commentary of Libanius 1–5 by P. Wolf (1967).

[16] *Plato's Seventh Letter* (1966), partly based on H. Cherniss, *The Riddle of the Early Academy* (1945): cf. the review by M. Isnardi Parente, *Rivista critica di storia della filosofia* 22 (1967) 90–94. K. von Fritz, *Platon in Sizilien* (1968), which appeared after my lectures had been delivered, defends the authenticity of the letter. Among earlier studies notice H. Gomperz, *Platons Selbstbiographie* (1928); G. Pasquali, *Le lettere di Platone* (1938); A. Maddalena, *Platone: Lettere* (1948).

know of any autobiographical letter comparable to Plato's *Seventh Letter* before Plato. I am reluctant to admit that forgery preceded reality in the matter of autobiographical letters. The letter seems to me an exceptional creation by an exceptional man, namely Plato. The second argument is that in terms of political history the *Seventh Letter* does not make much sense after Timoleon's success in Syracuse. Edelstein thinks that, when the author of *Letter 7* expressed his fears about the decline of the Greek population in Sicily, he knew of Timoleon's repopulation policy. But the dramatic appeal of *Letter 7* and the even more dramatic one on the same subject in *Letter 8* are intelligible only if prior to Timoleon. They explain why Timoleon had to act. It is even conceivable that Timoleon was inspired to act by Plato. I am much more hesitant about the philosophic sections of the letter. I must believe a great Platonic scholar like Edelstein—and of course his predecessors—when he tells me that Plato says something very un-Platonic in the *Seventh Letter*. And yet I am not convinced that for a letter to be un-Platonic is evidence of its not having been written by Plato. We have no other comparable letter by Plato and we cannot say how he would have written about his philosophical ideas in a context which was not one of philosophic research, but of personal self-defense and of practical policy. We may remind ourselves that K. Latte persuaded many scholars by his observation that Sallust's letters are not authentic because they are so Sallustian.[17] May we not suspect that the converse is also true, that Plato's *Letter 7* is authentic because it is so un-Platonic? Besides, old philosophers tend to prepare surprises for their students by saying new and unexpected, even embarrassing, things. Old Kant, old Bergson, old Croce are examples. Connoisseurs of Croce asked themselves more than once in Croce's last period whether what he wrote was true Croce. Like Giorgio Pasquali, I am struck by the series of depressing admissions which *Letter 7* contains. Plato admits to having been much

[17] *Journ. Rom. Studies* 27 (1937) 300.

nearer to Dionysius than to Dio. He recognizes his inability
to defend Dio's material interests. He admits that in the
meeting at Olympia in 360 he virtually refused to support
Dio. This is a dignified and total acknowledgement of failure
which is hard to conceive from the pen of a disciple of Plato,
whereas it is entirely in keeping with Plato's courage to face
his own failures.

Thus I believe that Plato's *Letter 7* is autobiography and
not biography: it is by Plato and not by some younger contemporary interested in Plato. In any case it is a remarkable
attempt to combine reflections on eternal problems and personal experiences. We have neither the letters (if letters they
were) of Empedocles to Pausanias nor those of Alcmaeon of
Croton (Diogenes Laertius 8.60 and 83), and we know too
little about the epistolography of the Hellenistic period.
Autobiographical letters of the fourth century such as the
letters of Timonidas of Leucas to Speusippus on the expedition of Dio (Plutarch *Dio* 35) probably covered only political
events without touching on intellectual experiences. We cannot, therefore, see the exact place of Plato's letter in the
history of ancient autobiographical production. But one
vaguely feels the Platonic precedent in Epicurus, Seneca, and
perhaps St. Paul. The letter as a conveyor of basic experiences
of one's own life was created in the fourth century B.C., at
least as far as the Greeks were concerned; and Plato seems to
have played a conspicuous part in the creation.[18]

V

The importance that biographical and autobiographical
experiments assumed in the fourth century is confirmed by
the interplay of biography and historiography in Theopompus' *Philippica*. Even the title shows that Theopompus
abandoned the Thucydidean scheme he had followed in the

[18] To my knowledge the survey by J. Sykutris, "Epistolographie," in *RE*
Suppl. 5, 186–220, is still unsurpassed. On St. Paul, P. Wendland, *Die urchrist-
lichen Literaturformen* (2nd–3rd ed. 1912) 342–346.

Hellenica and organized his account of contemporary events around a person: Philip of Macedon. The surviving fragments of the work, however insufficient, show what part Philip's virtues and vices played in Theopompus' history. Theopompus declared that Philip was a great man, the greatest man of Europe. Yet Philip had damaged himself and his cause by private vices. The emphasis on biography implied attention to psychology and gave a strong moral tone to historiography.[19] As Dionysius of Halicarnassus observed, judges in Hades must conduct their trials in the style of Theopompus (*Letter to Pompey* 6).

Within the general structure of his work Theopompus inserted long excursuses with many biographical details. This applies especially to the end of book 10 dedicated to Athenian demagogues. What Theopompus had to say about Athenian politicians was a gift to later biographers. We can still notice one palpable case of imitation: Cornelius Nepos and Plutarch talk about the princely style of Cimon in almost the same terms. Neither of them quotes Theopompus, but we have a verbatim report from Theopompus' book 10 in Athenaeus 12.533a–c which leaves no doubt as to the source of their accounts. Theopompus paved the way for Hellenistic biographers also in the sense that he examined in his digressions the lives of many men of the same kind. He has yet another excursus on religious prophets. He anticipates the typological interest of Hellenistic biographers.

Ephorus would provide confirmation of what we have said about Theopompus, though on a minor scale. Histories of Alexander and of the Diadochi are clear developments of historiography centred on individuals. It would, however, be wrong to conclude that even for a short period biography was indistinguishable from history. History went on being concerned with political events, even when they were guided and dominated by one man: biographical experiments turned on the personal life of the individual.

[19] For a different, valuable interpretation of Theopompus, W. R. Connor, *Greek, Roman and Byzantine Studies* 8 (1967) 133–154.

When Aristotle said in the *Poetics* (chap. 9, 1451b10) that the business of history is the particular, τί 'Αλκιβιάδης ἔπραξεν ἢ τί ἔπαθεν, what Alcibiades did or suffered, he may well have had in mind these biographical developments of the historiography of the fourth century. As Professor Homeyer acutely suggested,[20] he may have had in mind particularly the excursus on Alcibiades in book 10 of Theopompus' *Philippica*. But this passage of the *Poetics* does not imply an approach to history in a strictly biographical sense —as if historiography were biography. It is one thing to say that history means what Alcibiades did or suffered; it is another thing to say that the business of the historian is to write the biography of Alcibiades. Even Thucydides, the least biographical of historians, could be analysed in terms of the actions he attributed to Cleon or to Nicias or to Alcibiades, though admittedly it would be a partial analysis. No one, however, could interpret Thucydides' history as being based on biography. I cannot read into Aristotle's words more than a criterion for differentiating history from tragedy. I would not conclude from his words that Aristotle did not make a distinction between history and biography.[21]

The real question is rather whether Aristotle had any clear idea of biography. This can pertinently be asked when we turn to Peripatetic biography. Before Aristotle, I would say that there were experiments of a biographical and autobiographical kind which normally were kept outside political historiography as transmitted to the fourth century in the models of Herodotus and Thucydides.

[20] *Klio* 41 (1963) 146.
[21] Cf. the discussion by R. Weil, *Aristote et l'histoire* (1960) 163–178. The Isocratean encomium was fashionable about 330–320 B.C., if it is true that Theodectes wrote about Alexander of Epirus and Philiscus about the contemporary Lycurgus (Olympiodorus, *in Plat. Gorg.* 515 c) according to this model.

IV   From Aristotle to the Romans

I

The intellectual atmosphere of Athens changed after the Macedonian victory of 338 B.C. Macedonian rule meant the end both of Platonic mythmaking and of Isocratean rhetoric. There was no more experimentation on the borders between reality and fiction. The inventiveness which had characterized so much of Greek intellectual life in the first part of the fourth century was replaced by a new attitude of analysis and stocktaking. Plato was replaced by Aristotle, Isocrates by Demetrius of Phalerum. The world was becoming bigger every day owing to Alexander's conquests and the adventures of his immediate successors. But the intellectuals who had been left behind by Alexander were not in a mood of uncontrolled elation. Menander became the representative of Athenian society in the generation after Alexander: his characters, and Theophrastus' characters, are Greek, rather provincially so. Aristotle himself never recognized the empire built by his pupil as a form of political community worth studying. His search for facts to serve his philosophy was hellenocentric, sober, punctuated by that indefinable touch of irony and sadness which is the mark of Aristotelian genius. He had no use for the experiments in artistic, intuitive biography which had been a speciality of Plato and other Socratics. But it was not immediately obvious whether he and his pupils would replace the discarded forms of biography by new ones.

II

The general attitude of Aristotle and of his school towards historical research requires some definition. Aristotle had little sympathy with ordinary historiography, as he knew it. His words in chapter 9 of the *Poetics* are clear enough: "Poetry is something more scientific and serious than history, because poetry tends to give general truths, while history gives particular facts" (transl. W. Hamilton Fyfe). But chapter 23 of the same *Poetics* is less clear, and textual corruption has often been suspected. On any reading the passage is critical of historiography, "where what is required is an exposition not of a single piece of action, but of a single period of time, showing all that within the period befell one or more persons, events that have a merely casual relation to each other." D. M. Pippidi in a remarkable paper[1] tried to show that Aristotle made an exception for Thucydides in his condemnation of historians. One would like to believe Pippidi, but there is no evidence that Thucydides—whom Aristotle of course knew, yet never mentioned by name—was an exception for Aristotle.

What Aristotle's immediate pupils and continuators thought about history we simply do not know. Theophrastus commended Herodotus and Thucydides for their style. His opinion is reported by Cicero, *Orator* 12.39: "ab his historia commota est, ut auderet uberius quam superiores et ornatius dicere." This is not very helpful. The key to the attitude of the early Peripatetics to history was in the dialogue περὶ ἱστορίας by Praxiphanes: the key was lost with the dialogue itself. All we know of this dialogue is a mysterious sentence reported by Marcellinus, the biographer of Thucydides (chap. 29). According to Praxiphanes, Thucydides remained obscure as long as Archelaus (king of Macedon) lived, but became famous afterwards. The temptation to eliminate the word Archelaus is strong: Wilamowitz succumbed to it.[2] The sen-

---

[1] *Mélanges J. Marouzeau* (Paris 1948) 483–490.
[2] *Hermes* 12 (1877) 353 = *Kl. Schriften* 3 (1969) 27.

tence becomes innocently sensible after the operation: "Thucydides remained obscure as long as he lived, but after his death became famous." Innocence is no sign of authenticity: Archelaus must remain in Praxiphanes' fragment even if we no longer understand his presence. As the commentary by Poppo–Stahl observes in a sentence of general validity: "Praestat enim se nescientem fateri quam hariolari." All we learn from Marcellinus' text is that Thucydides played a part in Praxiphanes' dialogue. Perhaps he was chosen to represent history.[3]

What is less commonly observed, however, is that Aristotle did not merely express criticism of history as he knew it. He worked with all his forces, at least in the last years of his life, to overcome what he judged to be the shortcomings of ordinary historical writing. He tried to stimulate such historical research as he could accept as useful. He organized the collection of facts to answer precise questions: he replaced the narration of unrelated facts by a systematic analysis. He collected facts relating to culture and political institutions in order to give his own philosophy an empirical foundation. He took historical facts to be similar to natural facts and collected them in the same way under the same name of *historia*. A sophisticated example of how his mind worked is his application of historical research to deliberative eloquence. If a speaker wanted to give advice on war and peace, he had, according to a well-known passage in Aristotle's *Rhetorics* (1.4.1360a), to make an enquiry into the results of wars carried on not only by his own state, but also by others.

Aristotle's position can be compared with that of Bayle and Leibniz, who in the seventeenth century tried to overcome historical Pyrrhonism by a new type of historical research founded upon documents. Like Leibniz and Bayle, Aristotle turned to a pre-existing antiquarian tradition for help against contemporary historical writing. Literature on discoveries,

[3] Cf. K. O. Brink, *Class. Quart.* 40 (1946) 11–26; W. Aly, *RE* XXII, 1776–1777; F. Wehrli, *Die Schule des Aristoteles* 9 (1957) p. 98 F 18; p. 112.

on the history of music, of philosophy, and of science existed before him. He himself perfected some of the pre-existing research, for instance on political institutions, on the customs of the barbarians, on the lists of game winners. Other subjects he left to his pupils. Theophrastus studied the history of systems of physics and metaphysics, Eudemus the history of mathematics and astronomy, Meno the history of medicine.

The question has therefore to be asked whether biography had a place of its own in the systematic search for historical facts which Aristotle organized to serve his own philosophy.[4]

Aristotle himself never wrote biographies, nor did any of his most illustrious pupils, such as Theophrastus. But this is not in itself a sufficient argument to exclude biography from the new Aristotelian approach to historical research. There is abundant evidence that the Peripatos took an interest in biography. The difficulties which surround that interest are more complex.

Paradoxically, the first difficulty is in the obvious delight which Aristotle and his pupils took in anecdotes. Anecdotes can be enjoyed in themselves or can be a part of an argument or ingredients of a biography. The nature of our evidence makes it very hard to decide what in each case is the function of the anecdotes in the works of Aristotle and his pupils.

The difficulty is less great in Aristotle because we have the complete texts of many of his works and can see his anecdotes in context. Readers of his *Athenaion Politeia* know that its anecdotes—such as that on Pisistratus and the Hymettus farmer—are told for their own sakes. They are not really part of an argument. The same can be said of many other biographical remarks and stories found in Aristotle's more theoretical works. My favourite example of the irrelevant

---

[4] See K. O. Brink, art. "Peripatos" in *RE* Suppl. 7, 899–949, and the Italian edition of E. Zeller, *La filosofia dei Greci* II, 6 (1966, appendices by A. Plebe). All the texts of the early Peripatetics in F. Wehrli, *Die Schule des Aristoteles*; vol. 10 (1st ed., 1959) includes an invaluable survey "Der Peripatos in vorchristlicher Zeit." On Clearchus cf. now L. Robert, *Comptes Rendus Acad. Inscript.*, 1968, 421–457.

anecdote in Aristotle is his characterization of Hippodamus of Miletus at the beginning of a lengthy discussion of Hippo- damus' theories (*Politics* 2.1267b22). According to Aristotle, Hippodamus son of Euryphon was a Milesian, "who invented town planning and laid out Piraeus and had odd theories about other aspects of life which he liked to make himself known for: accounts of his foibles mention his long hair and expensive personal possessions and also the cheap but warm clothes he wore in summer as well as in winter, and his desire to be an expert in all the sciences." The cheap yet warm clothes that Hippodamus paraded not only in winter, but also in summer, can hardly have struck Aristotle as an argument against Hippodamus' political philosophy.

The works of Aristotle's pupils, with the exception of Theophrastus, are known to us only from chance quotations of later writers. When given an anecdote we are seldom in a position to decide whether it was part of an argument or of a biography.

Some facts, however, are indisputable. First, the Aristotel- ians were interested in anecdotes illustrating virtues and vices for use in their monographs on individual qualities: Hera- clides Ponticus, for instance, wrote monographs on piety and justice. More specifically, the Peripatetics were interested in the difference between contemplative life, active life, and sensual life. The Greeks had always been sensitive to the variety of individual inclinations. As Archilochus had said: ἀλλ' ἄλλος ἄλλῳ καρδίην ἰαίνεται (frag. 41 Diehl), which Mr. J. M. Edmonds translates "but various are the things which cheer men's hearts." The Peripatetics brought order into this variety with their books περὶ βίων, the best known of which seem to have been by Clearchus and Dicaearchus.[5]

Secondly, the Aristotelians were interested in individual writers. Books περὶ Σαπφοῦς, περὶ Στησιχόρου, περὶ Πινδάρου, and so forth, are common in the bibliography of the Peripatos. But these books do not appear to have been biographies. As F. Leo was the first to see, they were historical interpretations of selected passages from one classical author.[6] No doubt they were full of references to true or imaginary details of the author's life. Thanks to Athenaeus, we can form at least some idea of the works about poets by the very fertile Chamaeleon, who seems to have belonged to the first generation of the Peripatos. Chamaeleon was prone to infer the personal circumstances of his poets from what they wrote. Thus poems by Sappho and Anacreon were used as evidence of their love affairs. Aeschylus was not only the first to introduce drunkards into tragedy, but wrote while under the influence of alcohol: a motto by Sophocles was quoted in confirmation. Corinthian customs were adduced to explain why Pindar mentioned *hetairai* in poems celebrating Corinthian winners. All this represented a contribution to the technique of biographical research which cannot be underrated either on the positive or on the negative side. Hellenistic *érudits* had little direct evidence for the lives of archaic, or even of classical, poets. The technique of extracting information about the lives of writers from their works was both a legitimate and an extremely dangerous substitute for direct information. It helped Hellenistic erudition out of an impasse, but it also opened the door to the most irresponsible exploitation of literary documents. What we must emphasize here is that even this enormous accumulation of biographical details in commentaries on poets does not necessarily imply the existence of full-fledged biographies. Didymus' work on Demosthenes, περὶ Δημοσθένους, a portion of which was recovered in a Berlin papyrus published by Diels and Schubart in 1904, is a later (first century B.C.) specimen of the same literary genre. It contains a great many biographical details

---

[6] With special clarity in "Didymos Περὶ Δημοσθένους," *Nachrichten Götting. Gesell.* 1904, 254–261 = *Ausgewählte Kleine Schriften* II (1960) 387–394. Cf. R. Pfeiffer, *History of Classical Scholarship* (1968) 146 n. 2: " . . . this genre was, so to speak, discovered by F. Leo in his review of Didymus." Leo himself emphasized that there were exceptions to his rule.

about Demosthenes, but of course it is no biography.[7] Even in the case of books with such titles as "About Illustrious Men," whose prototype was by Neanthes of Cyzicus (about 275 B.C. ?), we remain in doubt whether they were a series of short biographies or a collection of anecdotes about illustrious men.

Thirdly, Peripatetic philosophers were interested in describing and evaluating the various philosophic schools. This involved them in collecting anecdotes about philosophers, but not necessarily in writing biographies. We are naturally inclined to think that Dicaearchus wrote biographies of philosophers because he certainly went into details of the lives of Socrates, Plato, and Aristotle. Besides, he wrote the celebrated "Life of Greece"; and we would expect him also to have written the lives of certain individuals of Greece. Yet no biography is quoted as coming from his pen. Diogenes Laertius (3.4) reports a detail about Plato as found ἐν πρώτῳ περὶ βίων by Dicaearchus, which would imply that this biographical detail belonged to a work on the different types of life. Works on the different philosophic schools were used in the struggles between the schools. The very purpose for which they were exploited makes one reluctant to conclude that they were biographical. Attacks on doctrinal tenets must have been freely mixed with attacks on individuals, in unknown proportion. Anecdotes served to characterize modes of life, of thought, of style. If Phainias or Phanias of Eresus in his book on the Socratics said that Aristippus was the first of the Socratics to pay for tuition and to make money by teaching (Diogenes Laertius 2.65), the story must have been meant to characterize, or perhaps to discredit, the hedonistic inclinations of Aristippus. Books of this type on philosophic schools, though probably first written in the Peripatos, soon became the common patrimony of Hellenistic culture. The Epicurean Idomeneus' book "On the Socratics" can

---

[7] P. Foucart, "Étude sur Didymos d'après un papyrus de Berlin," *Mém. Acad. Inscriptions,* 38, 1 (1909), is still the fundamental work.

hardly have been other than a hostile book against the Socratics, just as centuries later Philodemus wrote a hostile book against the Stoics with the anodyne title "On the Stoics."

Fourthly, and lastly, the Peripatetics had a part in producing the various types of collections of anecdotes which became a prominent feature of the Hellenistic and Latin literatures. Certain varieties of this erudition were current before Aristotle. Books on discoveries (*heuremata*) were written in the late fifth century and early fourth century.[8] Isocrates (*Panegyricus* 10) knew the genre in about 380 B.C. Anecdotes on strange events and personalities (*paradoxa, thaumasia*) were collected by Theopompus and perhaps by Ephorus. Collections of apt answers or remarks (*apophthegmata, gnomai, chreiai*) were another genre: as we have seen, Xenophon (*Hellenica* 2.3.56) knew that *apophthegmata* were unsuitable for insertion into a historical work. "Examples" (*paradeigmata*)—that is, memorable precedents to be quoted or copied when occasion arises— are as old as Homer (*Iliad* 5.381). The term *paradeigma* is known to the fourth-century author of the *Rhetorica ad Alexandrum* (1429a21)—Anaximenes?—as an ingredient of rhetoric. The second book of the *Oeconomica* attributed to Aristotle is specifically devoted to expedients in money matters. Later, in the first century B.C., Parthenius wrote an anthology of love stories. Collections of military stratagems fall into this category. Books of anecdotes on the deaths of illustrious men can be traced from the Peripatetic Phainias of Eresus to the *Exitus illustrium virorum* by Titinius Capito in the first century A.D. and even to Lactantius' *De mortibus persecutorum* in the fourth century. Indeed *exempla* became very popular among the Romans. Cornelius Nepos, Hyginus (Augustus' freedman), and Augustus himself made their collections. Valerius Maximus, who wrote under Tiberius,

---

[8] Cf. the admirable article by K. Thraede, "Erfinder," in *Reallex. für Antike und Christentum* 5 (1962), esp. 1191–1232. Add to the bibl. L. Cracco Ruggini, "Eforo nello Pseudo-Aristotele, *Oec.* II?" in *Athenaeum* 44 (1966) 199–237, 45 (1967) 3–88.

has survived with his *Facta et dicta memorabilia* to give us a precise idea of the genre.

In theory there should be no difficulty in recognizing the difference between any of these literary works and proper Hellenistic biographies. But in practice fragments are often insufficient to give us an indication of the exact nature of lost books. Mere titles can be even more misleading. Furthermore, genuine borderline cases disturb the neatness of the picture. Satyrus' life of Euripides has features in common with the above-mentioned commentaries (the so-called περί literature) of Chamaeleon and Didymus. Later Greek biographies, such as the anonymous life of the philosopher Secundus and Lucian's life of Demonax (second century A.D.), are mainly made up of sayings (*apophthegmata, chreiai*): biography is here the framework for a collection of pointed remarks and definitions. In all these cases the difficulty of seeing the dividing line between a collection of anecdotes and biography proper is doubled by the difficulty in determining the exact purpose of the biographical enquiry.

III

The circle of the undisputed biographers within the Peripatetic School is much more restricted. However, we must emphasize again and again that our ignorance may well mislead us in the evaluation of Peripatetic biography. St. Jerome offers a precise point of reference in the preface to his *De viris illustribus,* which must derive its information from Suetonius and which introduces as Suetonius' predecessors among the Greeks: "apud Graecos Hermippus Peripateticus, Antigonus Carystius, Satyrus doctus vir et omnium longe doctissimus Aristoxenus Musicus." Thus Aristoxenus, Hermippus, Antigonus of Carystus, and Satyrus are quoted as Greek biographers.

Three of the four names are connected with the Peripatetic School: Aristoxenus, Hermippus, and Satyrus; and therefore are enough to prove that the Peripatos had a leading part in shaping Hellenistic biography. Only Antigonus of Carystus was clearly outside this school. Yet we must immediately remark that only one of the three Peripatetics, Aristoxenus of Tarentum, belongs to the first generation of Aristotle's pupils—and Aristoxenus was no conventional Aristotelian. We come nearer to the problems of the origins and of the limits of the influence of so-called Peripatetic biography if we take the origins and development of this extravagant man into consideration.

Aristoxenus of Tarentum, who must have been born about 370 B.C., had received a full training as a Pythagorean before he went over to the Peripatos in obscure circumstances. About 343 B.C. he had the opportunity to meet in Corinth Dionysius the Younger, then an exile from Syracuse, and to compare notes with him about Pythagorean behaviour. He learned from Dionysius the story of the Pythagorean friends Damon and Phintias which all of us in our school days had to translate either from the Greek of Diodorus and Iamblichus, from the Latin of Cicero or from the German of Schiller. By 322, on the death of Aristotle, Aristoxenus could consider himself qualified to succeed his master in the headship of the Peripatos, and he took offence when Theophrastus was preferred to him. It is doubtful whether he remained a Peripatetic after that. In any case he never concealed his sympathies for Pythagoras and his dislike of Plato. He even had something unpleasant to say about Aristotle as a man, if it is true that he insinuated that Aristotle built up his own school at a time when he was able to take advantage of Plato's absence. Plato he considered a plagiarist of Pythagoras.[9] Even his Socrates was, to say the least, unconventional: a man who could get very angry and did not mind turning an honest penny by lending money. Just because this is an unusual Socrates, we relish the picture and would like to be able to

[9] The evidence in the edition of Aristoxenus by F. Wehrli. O. Gigon, *Vita Aristotelis Marciana* (1962) 18, is more doubtful about Aristoxenus' attitude towards Plato.

agree with A. von Mess, who hailed Aristoxenus as the true biographer of Socrates.[10] But ancient philosophers were not supposed to get angry or to lend money; and it is difficult to escape the conclusion that Aristoxenus brought an element of malice into his picture of the Socratic schools. Aristoxenus made himself the biographer of Pythagoras and Archytas on the one side, and of Socrates and Plato on the other, to compare styles of life and tenets. He gives the impression of having had greater sympathy for his earlier than for his later masters, though on the whole he was far more respectful to Aristotle than he was to Plato. He accompanied his biography of Pythagoras with a study (probably in another book) of the Pythagorean style of life, a sensitive and discriminating description of a Pythagorean community.

Enough has been said to show that it would be far too simple to present Aristoxenus' biographies as the product of a conventional Aristotelian upbringing. They were a personal achievement inspired by his peculiar position between two schools: the Pythagorean school from which he had moved and the Peripatetic school of which he was an uneasy follower. He was a cosmopolite and presented Pythagoras as a man of Etruscan origins who went to learn wisdom from the Chaldaean Zoratas, that is Zarathustra. He was aware and proud of the fact that Pythagorean doctrines acquired followers among Lucanians, Messapians, Peucetians, and Romans.[11] Perhaps his belief that Pythagoras was an Etruscan had something to do with the popularity of Pythagoreanism in central Italy. We may even suspect that the Pythagorean tradition, with its strong emphasis on the personality and the example of the master, prepared Aristoxenus to become a biographer. But I do not think it wise to labour this point, because we know almost nothing about Pythagorean tradition before Aristoxenus. The sensitiveness to moral values and to human situa-

---

[10] *RhM* 71 (1916) 79.
[11] E. Gabba, in *Entretiens Fondation Hardt*, XIII: *Les origines de la république romaine* (1967) 157–163.

tions is very much Aristoxenus' own. In the conflict between different tenets and personalities, to none of which he owed complete allegiance, he developed his gift for observation and his capacity for unifying episodes within a biographical framework. He has the tone of a man who has seen too much to take a narrow view of human attitudes. In the story of Damon and Phintias the tyrant Dionysius is by no means the villain. In the description of the encounter between the austere Archytas and the voluptuous Polyarchus, which is preserved in Athenaeus, both protagonists are treated fairly: "Among the envoys sent by Dionysius the Younger to the city of Tarentum was Polyarchus, nicknamed the High-Liver, a man entirely devoted to physical pleasures, and this not merely in act, but also by his own confession. He was an acquaintance of Archytas and not an utter stranger to philosophic teachings; he frequented the temple-enclosures and would walk about with the other followers of Archytas, listening to the discussion . . ." (12.545, transl. C. B. Gulick).

Aristotle did not cross the bridge from anecdote to biography. Nor did Theophrastus, with all his attention to human character. Though other Peripatetics have claims worth considering in this connection, I think (basically in agreement with F. Leo, though for other reasons) that Aristoxenus is most likely to have been the first to write biography in the Peripatos. He must have picked up the loose threads of fifth-century biography, availed himself of the variety of biographical techniques displayed in the early fourth century, and appreciated the new trends of erudite research favoured by Aristotle. He was the man to produce a new blend: learned, yet worldly; attentive to ideas, yet gossipy. Perhaps he was also the first to make anecdotes an essential part of biography. We are so used to considering anecdotes the natural condiment of biography that we forget that just as there can be anecdotes without biography so there can be biography without anecdotes. I suspect that we owe to Aristoxenus the notion that a good biography is full of good anecdotes.

IV

If Aristoxenus was the first Peripatetic biographer, we may
well ask ourselves whether his success was immediate—both
inside and outside the Peripatos.

Now Clearchus wrote an encomium of Plato, and it has
been suggested that Clearchus wanted to give an answer to
the naughty things Aristoxenus had said about Plato. This is
not impossible. But the title "encomium" connects the work
of Clearchus with Speusippus' encomium of Plato (Diogenes
Laertius 4.5), and Speusippus in turn seems to have imitated
Isocrates' encomium of Euagoras. Certainly Clearchus followed Speusippus in making Plato the son of Apollo (Diogenes Laertius 3.2). Clearchus' encomium of Plato therefore
seems to have belonged to an older type of biographical
writing. Even if Clearchus wrote with polemical intent
against Aristoxenus, his encomium of Plato and Aristoxenus'
life of Plato were probably not biographies of the same type.

Demetrius of Phalerum is a much more difficult case.
Dionysius of Halicarnassus (*De Demosthene* 53) seems to state
that he wrote a biography of Demosthenes, but he is not
supported by the other evidence. It is more probable that
Demetrius discussed episodes of Demosthenes' life in his
books on rhetoric. Diogenes Laertius (5.81) mentions a book
Socrates by Demetrius and quotes three times from an "Apology of Socrates" by the same Demetrius. Plutarch (*Aristides*
1 and 27) quotes biographical details from the book *Socrates*.
It is probable that *Socrates* and the "Apology of Socrates"
were the same work. But it is not clear whether this work was
a biography. If it was, it might have been an answer to Aristoxenus.

Another name to be considered among those who may have
been influenced by Aristoxenus is Phainias (or Phanias) of
Eresus. He was a pupil of Aristotle and a special friend of
Theophrastus; and he is described by Plutarch (*Themistocles*
13) as a philosopher not unversed in historical writing. One of
his historical works was a direct development of a suggestion

in Aristotle's *Politics* (1311a25): he wrote on the elimination of tyrants as a consequence of revenge. Tyrannies seem to have attracted him. He also wrote a monograph "On the Sicilian Tyrants." His works included monographs on the Socratics and on the prytanes of his native town Eresus. The fragments show the typical Peripatetic interest in details, but it is uncertain whether any of the works so far mentioned was biographical. If the work on the tyrants of Sicily was modelled on Theopompus' excursus on the demagogues, it was probably anecdotal rather than strictly biographical. Plutarch says, however, that some of his biographical details on Solon and Themistocles are derived from Phainias. These present a real problem. The details about Solon are perhaps not very impressive, but those about Themistocles have rightly attracted attention as fine specimens of biographical style. The famous scene of the arrival of Themistocles at the Persian court is explicitly attributed to Phainias by Plutarch. L. Bodin[12] and R. Laqueur[13] assumed that Phainias wrote a full biography of Themistocles and proceeded on this assumption to a reconstruction of Phainias' biographical work. The very assumption from which they started is of course doubtful. Neither Plutarch nor anybody else tells us that Phainias wrote a biography of Themistocles—or of Solon. The episodes that Plutarch reports are excellent samples of what a biography might be, but these samples may have belonged to a collection of anecdotes. In other words, we are faced again by what I feel to be a major difficulty in studying Peripatetic biography, namely the difficulty of separating anecdotes from biography. In the present state of our knowledge it would be absurd to deny altogether that Phainias wrote biographies; but it is a waste of time to try to guess what sort of biography Phainias may have written, since we cannot be certain that there even was biography by Phainias.

What emerges from our enquiry is a confirmation of our

---

[12] *Rev. Ét. Grecques* 28–30 (1915–1917).
[13] *RE* s.v. "Phainias."

hypothesis that, unless Dicaearchus' περὶ βίων was a collection of biographies, Aristoxenus had no rival as a biographer in the first generation of the Peripatos. Extensive practice of learned biography, both inside and outside the Peripatos, we find only in the second or third generation after Aristotle. The three names of Hermippus, Satyrus, and Antigonus of Carystus quoted by St. Jerome belong to the second part of the third century B.C. Both Hermippus and Satyrus are called Peripatetics. In some sense they must have been followers of Aristotle. What we know of Hermippus at any rate would rather make him a pupil of Callimachus and an exploiter of the materials collected by him. No doubt Callimachus' *Pinakes* may ultimately have been inspired by the methods of cataloguing Aristotle's library: at least Strabo (13.608) states that the organization of the library of Alexandria imitated that of Aristotle's. But Callimachus is not the man to be reduced to the role of a pupil of Aristotle.[14]

Hermippus, who was born in Smyrna, lived in Alexandria about 200 B.C. He used Callimachus' files for his biographies, including archaic legislators, the Seven Wise Men, Pythagoras, Gorgias, Isocrates, Aristotle, and their respective pupils. His interest in the frivolous, the morbid (death scenes), the paradoxical is well established: he went all out to captivate his readers by learned sensationalism. (Compare also the summaries by Heraclides Lembus in *POxy* XI 1367). He continued the Peripatetic practice of grouping men of the same profession in the same book. The lawgivers were included in at least six books, the Seven Wise Men in at least four books of his biographies.[15] He was careful to indicate school affiliations (Dionysius Halicarnassensis *De Isaeo* 1.1). He accepted what must have been a suggestion from an earlier (Peripatetic or

[14] O. Regenbogen, *RE* s.v. "Pinax"; R. Pfeiffer, *History of Classical Scholarship*, 127–134.

[15] F. E. Adcock, *Cambridge Histor. Journ.* 2 (1927) 106 on Hermippus and the lawgivers. I. Düring, *Class. et Mediaev.* 17 (1956) 11; A.-H. Chroust, *Rev. Ét. Grecques* 77 (1964) 53; R. Pfeiffer, *History of Classical Scholarship*, 129, with other bibl. On Neanthes' priority, R. Laqueur, *RE* s.v. "Neanthes."

Jewish?) scholar that Pythagoras had imported Jewish thought into Greece: Flavius Josephus was of course pleased with that admission (*Contra Apionem* 1.22.163).

Satyrus was probably born later than Hermippus, if he is identical with the author of a book on the demes of Alexandria which presupposes the reforms of Ptolemy IV at the end of the third century. The recent publication of a new fragment of this work has not thrown any new light on its date and authorship (*POxy* XXVII 2465). On the other hand, Satyrus the biographer is certain to have lived before Ptolemy VI (about 150 B.C.), because Heraclides Lembus who lived under Ptolemy VI made an epitome not only of Hermippus' but also of Satyrus' biographies. It was a surprise to discover from Papyrus Oxyrhynchus 1176, which was published in 1912, that Satyrus wrote biographies in the form of a dialogue. Biographies in dialogue form were previously known only from late antiquity, in Sulpicius Severus, Palladius, and Gregory the Great's life of St. Benedict. Aristotle's dialogue on poets is not quite a precedent for Satyrus. Nor is Cicero's *Brutus* entirely comparable, though F. Leo declared it to be the nearest analogue to Satyrus' work.[16] Satyrus undoubtedly intended to write biographies. The subscription of Papyrus Oxyrhynchus 1176 reads: "Book Six of the catalogue (?) of the lives of Satyrus including Aeschylus, Sophocles, and Euripides." This must be said, because A. Dihle reports a suggestion by K. Latte that Satyrus' life of Euripides belonged to the literature on *problemata*: it was not true biography. The text of the papyrus, with its clear transition from a section dealing with the life to a section dealing with the death of the poet, seems to make the biographical intention unmistakable. Satyrus deduced many of his biographical details about Euripides from the text of Euripides' tragedies. This was good Peripatetic method, as we have seen. He also reflects the

---

[16] *Ausgewählte Kleine Schriften* II 368. Cicero may, however, have written in dialogue form his eulogy of the younger Cato: the strange statement of *Schol. Iuven.* 6, 338 p. 95 Wessner is well defended by C. P. Jones in a forthcoming article [*RhM* 113 (1970) 188–196].

interests of the school in literary history by linking the new comedy of Menander with Euripides.

The third man mentioned by St. Jerome, Antigonus of Carystus, had nothing to do with the Peripatos. He lived in the middle of the third century B.C., if he can be identified with the courtier of Attalus I, king of Pergamum. His profession was that of a bronze founder, and his literary activity was amateurish. In his youth he had been a pupil of the philosopher Menedemus, the originator of the Eretrian school. He imitated Aristoxenus in writing about philosophers either of the previous generation or of his own time: the Sceptics Pyrrho and Timon, the Academics Polemo, Crates, Crantor, and Arcesilaus, the Peripatetic Lyco; Menedemus, and finally Zeno of Citium, who died in 263. It would be optimistic to say, even after Wilamowitz' feat of reconstruction, that we know what Antigonus intended—if he intended anything.[17] He certainly showed curiosity and was very good at describing personal appearances. He drew a striking portrait of his master Menedemus, whose dinner parties were proverbially frugal.

We can add other names to those given by St. Jerome. One is Aristo of Ceos, probably the head of the Peripatos in the last part of the third century. He wrote on Heraclitus, Socrates, and Epicurus; and at least his book on Epicurus is explicitly called a life by Diogenes Laertius 10.14. The other is Sotion, who lived at Alexandria about 180 B.C. and wrote on the "Succession of Philosophers": a book which is assumed to have strongly influenced the organization of Diogenes Laertius' "Lives of Philosophers." I am not aware that Sotion had Peripatetic affiliations. Like Hermippus he seems to have exploited the files of Callimachus' *Pinakes*.

Three biographers of the Peripatetic school—Hermippus, Satyrus, and Aristo—face two biographers (Antigonus of Carystus and Sotion) who did not belong to the Peripatos. Of the three Peripatetics only one, Aristo, played an important

---

[17] Cf. O. Gigon in *Lexikon der Alten Welt,* s.v. "Biographie."

part in the school: he is also the least important as a biographer. As for Hermippus, we hardly know why he was called a Peripatetic. The connection between the Peripatos and biography is not so permanent and so close as we are often told, even if we confine ourselves to biographies of philosophers, artists, sages, and poets. If we agree to consider Aristoxenus, the dubious Aristotelian, the master of Peripatetic biography, we are obliged to conclude that there was a gap of at least one generation before his teaching produced pupils—and these pupils were by no means all members of the Peripatos.

The picture becomes even more blurred if we look at other aspects of biographical and autobiographical literature of the Hellenistic period.

We have seen that the type of biographical encomium created by Isocrates continued to be popular. Theopompus' encomia of Philip and Alexander of Macedon belong to this genre: so does Callisthenes' encomium of Hermias. If Clearchus expanded the encomium to cover the life of Plato, others undoubtedly developed it to cover the lives of generals and statesmen. Some encomia must have been very similar to political history, though the two were never confused. Polybius, who himself wrote an encomium of Philopoemen in three books, stated what one would expect to find in an encomium of this kind: "explaining who he and his family were and the nature of his training when young . . . enumerating his most famous actions." An encomium—Polybius went on—"demanded a summary and somewhat exaggerated account of his achievements" (10.21 = *FGrHist* 173). An extensive account of the period of education had to be followed by a selective report of political and military achievements. Ordinary history would hardly give space to the youth of a future general and would report diplomatic moves and military operations much more fully. This explains why many books on great men had a reference to education in their titles. Onesicritus' "How Alexander Was Educated" (ὡς Ἀλέξανδρος ἤχθη) is paralleled by the "Education of

Alexander" ('Αλεξάνδρου ἀγωγή) by Marsyas of Pella, who
had been one of Alexander's companions. In the third century
a Lysimachus wrote περὶ τῆς 'Αττάλου παιδείας, "About the
Education of Attalus I." Thus L. Pearson was wrong in
suggesting that· the title of Onesicritus' book should be
emended from ὡς 'Αλέξανδρος ἤχθη to ὡς 'Αλέξανδρος ἀνήχθη,
"How Alexander Marched On."[18]

The gap between this type of historical encomium and a
full biography of a king or of a general is so narrow that any
neat separation is impossible. Satyrus himself wrote on
Philip II and Dionysius the Younger of Syracuse; Neanthes
the Younger (about 200 B.C.) wrote on Attalus I; Asclepiades
Areiou on Demetrius of Phalerum; Timochares on one
Antiochus, perhaps Epiphanes or Sidetes, (*FGrHist* 165).
Sosylus notoriously wrote about Hannibal, a certain Posidonius on Perseus of Macedon (*FGrHist* 169). How far were
these biographies inspired by the Peripatos? How clearly can
we distinguish between such biographies and the books which
meant to tell political history in the form of a monograph
about an individual king? The memorialists of Alexander's
wars—Clitarchus, Ptolemy, and Aristobulus—the historians
of the Diadochoi and of the Hellenistic kings (such as
Timaeus on Pyrrhus, Demetrius of Byzantium on Antiochus
Soter and on Ptolemy Philadelphus) are in this ambiguous
position between biography and history. Surely it is impossible to try to enforce a rigid separation of biography
from the monograph centred on one man. As Richard
Reitzenstein showed in famous pages of his *Hellenistische
Wundererzählungen* (1906), the theory of historiography contained in Cicero's letter to Lucceius (*ad familiares* 5.12) applies
both to the biography and to the monograph centred on one
man ("Si uno in argumento unaque in persona mens tua tota
versabitur"). There is no reason to believe that Cicero re-
peated Peripatetic theory in this letter. But, even if he did, the
biographical practice which such a letter presupposes—

[18] *The Lost Histories of Alexander the Great* (1960) 89–90.

monographs on kings, generals, politicians—cannot be connected exclusively with Peripatetic circles. Satyrus is clearly the exception, not the rule, as a Peripatetic biographer of kings.[19]

The evidence so far available seems to justify the conclusion that Hellenistic biography is to be considered a Peripatetic speciality only in a limited sense. The great Aristotelian conception of a systematic exploration of the empirical world had not survived the first generation of the pupils. Biography soon ceased to have a specific function within the Peripatos. It remained closely connected with philology because questions of authenticity and interpretation of texts were inextricably connected with biography. It was also used by philosophers at large as a weapon against hostile schools. But more often biography provided entertainment for educated people who liked to know something about the lives of poets, philosophers, and kings. The type of life we call Peripatetic is the result of a sort of compromise. The basic interest in discovering a variety of human characters had a philosophic root, but the wealth of strange details, of piquant anecdotes, was ultimately meant to satisfy the curiosity of the common reader.

The extent and importance of Greek biographical literature of the second and first centuries B.C. is a matter for speculation. An example will show the inadequacy of our information. We should never have known that Eratosthenes wrote a book entitled *Arsinoe* if it had not been quoted once by Athenaeus 276a–c (*FGrHist* 241F16). The quotation shows beyond doubt that in about 215 B.C. Eratosthenes reported details of the life of Arsinoe III Philopator from personal knowledge.

---

[19] Another theory, in *Auctor ad Herennium* 1.8.13 and Cicero *De inventione* 1.19.27, makes a distinction between two kinds of narrative, one based on "negotia" (legendary, historical, and imaginary), the other on "personae." R. Reitzenstein, *Hellenistische Wundererzählungen* (1906) 94; K. Kerényi, *Die griechisch-orientalische Romanliteratur* (1927, 2nd ed. 1962) 2; S. Trenkner, *The Greek Novella in the Classical Period* (1958) 183, have taken the narrative based on "personae" to refer to, or at least to include, the novel. But these passages are not clear to me. Cf. also K. Barwick, *Hermes* 63 (1928) 261; F. Pfister, *Hermes* 68 (1933) 457.

He tells us that one day he was accompanying the queen when she met a crowd celebrating a Dionysiac festival and that she expressed disgust at it. As her husband, Ptolemy IV Philopator, was a great supporter of Dionysiac festivals, the story has its point. Perhaps there is a link between Eratosthenes' book on Arsinoe and the book of stories about her husband by Ptolemy son of Hegesarchus of Megalopolis, which gave much space to the king's devotion to Dionysus (*FGrHist* 161F2). But the exact nature of the book *Arsinoe* is unknown: it may have been a biography; more probably it was a learned discussion with a biographical, or perhaps rather autobiographical, background.

If the discovery of the Satyrus papyrus on Euripides glaringly exposed the lacunae of our information about Hellenistic biography, a more recent discovery underlined even more sharply the extent of our ignorance. *Papyrus Graeca Hauniensis* 6, published by T. Larsen in 1942, seems to contain short biographies of third century B.C. Ptolemies within the framework of a genealogical tree. Mario Segre—in a paper he had meant to be provisional, but which death in a Nazi camp made final—tried to prove that the author was under the influence of the Roman *imagines maiorum*. His theory is not convincing, but no better interpretation of the unusual text has yet been offered. Though the papyrus was written in the second century A.D., the text itself seems to be Hellenistic. It may provide (if it is a combination of genealogy with biography) the closest analogy I can think of to the *Ordo generis Cassiodororum* which the great Cassiodorus composed in the sixth century A.D.[20]

[20] M. Segre, "Una genealogia dei Tolemei e le imagines maiorum dei Romani," *Rend. Acc. Pontif. Archeol.* 19 (1942–1943) 269–280. Cf. A. Momigliano, *Class. Quart.* 44 (1950) 107–116; W. Steidle, *Sueton und die antike Biographie* (1951) 177; É. Will, *Histoire politique du monde hellénistique* I (1966) 211. The comparison with Cassiodorus is already in Segre. Cassiodorus' genealogical text, known to us from excerpts, was first edited by H. Usener under the title of *Anecdoton Holderi* (Bonn 1877). It was reprinted by Mommsen in his edition of *Cassiodori Variae*, p. v (*Mon. Germ. Hist., Auct. Antiquissimi* XII [1894]). More recent bibliography in my *Studies in Historiography* (1966) 205.

It would be splendid if we were able to resolve our doubts about the nature of Peripatetic biography by turning to a contemporary of the Emperor Augustus, Nicolaus of Damascus.[21] He was brought up as an Aristotelian and wrote an autobiography and a life of Augustus, of both of which we have unusually extensive fragments. At first sight, Nicolaus seems ideally suited to tell us what Peripatetic biography was like. Indeed his fragments show clear signs of his school allegiance: he describes both his own qualities and those of Augustus according to Aristotle's ethics. But his Aristotelianism is superficial. He is bent on writing a panegyric both of himself and of Augustus—and he is in many other ways remote from the scholarly habits of the Aristotelians. What is not encomiastic in his works is a straightforward account of political and social events in which I do not see anything specifically Aristotelian. His life of Augustus is the best preserved example of a biography of a king in the Hellenistic tradition. Clearly it depends to a large extent on Augustus' own autobiography, but Nicolaus interprets the data according to his own taste. The result, as far as we can judge, is a dynastic biography, its main emphasis on the devotion of Octavian to the memory of his adoptive father, Caesar. Plutarch may owe something of his biographical technique to Nicolaus.

It is virtually certain that not only the "Plutarchian" (chronologically ordered) but also the "Suetonian" (systematically ordered) type of biography existed in the Hellenistic period. Among "Suetonian" biographies, the abridged *Vita* of Sophocles, for instance, does not quote any authority later than the second century B.C. The *Vita Marciana* of

---

[21] Text with a fundamental commentary in Jacoby, *FGrHist* 90. A controversial interpretation by R. Laqueur in *RE* XVII, 1 (1936) 362–424. Cf. B. Z. Wacholder, *Nicolaus of Damascus* (1962), which tries to establish connections between Nicolaus' autobiography and Jewish writings. He has not convinced me, and I am doubtful about the analysis of Nicolaus' life of Augustus by W. Steidle, *Sueton und die antike Biographie* (1951) 133–140.

Aristotle—provided some patent accretions are eliminated (polemics against Aelius Aristides)—is likely to represent the substance of the biography Andronicus wrote about 70 B.C. to introduce his epoch-making edition of Aristotle. The recently discovered life of Pindar in a papyrus (*POxy* 2438) of the second century A.D. gives the impression of being an unadulterated summary of Hellenistic research. Even the composite biography of Thucydides which goes under the name of Marcellinus, though in its present form not earlier than the fifth century A.D., preserves the learned discussion which was going on at the time of Didymus (first century B.C.) about the mysterious family connections and about the equally mysterious death of the Athenian historian. These are random examples of "Suetonian" biographies, the substance of which must go back to Alexandrian erudition. But it is well to remind ourselves that none of the surviving "Suetonian" biographies (in their present form) belongs to the period before Augustus.

Furthermore, the evidence of the surviving texts is not sufficient to indicate when and how the diversification in the two types of biography took place. The name which F. Leo connected with the creation of the "Suetonian" biography (Heraclides Lembus in the second century B.C.) is not supported by any substantial proof. Indeed, we must doubt Leo's doctrine that the "Suetonian" scheme was originally reserved for biographies of literary and artistic personalities and was first applied to the emperors precisely by Suetonius. The Suetonian scheme is only a refinement of the systematic order of certain "encomia" of kings and generals. Two of the nonliterary biographies of Cornelius Nepos are nearer to the Suetonian than to the Plutarchian type (Epaminondas, Iphicrates). On the other hand, the literary biographies of the Ten Orators wrongly attributed to Plutarch can be forced into the Suetonian scheme only with considerable difficulty. The Suetonian type was better suited to the lives of writers and artists, as it allowed a systematic analysis of their personal qualities and of their works. But we have no reason to believe that it was ever restricted to the nonpolitical biography.[22]

Future research or perhaps future discoveries of texts will solve the problem of the origins of the Suetonian biography: at the moment a confession of ignorance is not out of place.

In any case we must not assume any great uniformity in Hellenistic biographies. Lives of poets could not be constructed like lives of philosophers; and lives of generals and kings were different from either. To write about men who had lived long ago was not the same thing as writing about contemporaries. Poets of the past had left few authentic memories. The fragments of the monument erected to Archilochus in his native Paros give us an idea of how Hellenistic scholars managed to build up biographies on the basis of inferences from poems, information from older chronicles, oral tradition, and imagination. The relation between poetry and life was in itself a problem which exercised ingenuity and encouraged perversity in the handling of the literary evidence. Philosophers had left behind disciples whose opinions had to be taken into account. Kings and generals had left their traces in general history; this was bound to affect their biographies.

More work must be done on this subject. Much can be learned from later biographies which used Hellenistic models. But the dangers of making inferences from later texts are obvious. Though, for instance, we know that Iamblichus directly or indirectly used Aristoxenus for his life of Pythagoras, Iamblichus' own neo-Platonic atmosphere is all-

---

[22] On "Suetonian" biography see F. Leo, *Griechisch-römische Biographie,* esp. 118–135 (the part he attributes to Heraclides Lembus on p. 135 is not clear to me); what Wilamowitz wrote in *Antigonos von Karystos* (1881) 88 is altogether different. Cf. A. Rostagni, *Suetonius De Poetis* (1944) XII–XXIV. For a critical evaluation of Leo's theory, W. Steidle, *Sueton und die antike Biographie*, 126–177, is particularly important. Cf. also G. Arrighetti, *Satiro, Vita di Euripide* (1964) 5–21. On Marcellinus see Bux, *RE* XIV 1450–1487. On Pindar's biography (*POxy* XXVI 2438), E. G. Turner, *Greek Papyri* (1968) 104–106, and G. Arrighetti, *Studi Class. Orient.* 16 (1967) 129–148 (who quotes Turner). The *Vita Marciana* of Aristotle is admirably edited by O. Gigon, Berlin 1962. H. Bloch, *Trans. Am. Phil. Ass.* 71 (1940) 27–39, showed how unoriginal Heraclides Lembus was.

pervasive: it does not allow safe conclusions about Aristoxenus.

V

At this stage I need hardly refute the opinion, made authori-
tative by F. Leo and Wilamowitz, that autobiography was
unknown to the Greeks.[23] The evidence for autobiographical
writing in the fifth and fourth centuries has been previously
considered. The fourth-century tradition of writing apologetic pamphlets to defend oneself remained alive under Alexander and afterwards. It is difficult to decide whether Dema-
des' apology was a forgery, as Jacoby maintains (*FGrHist* II
D, p. 641). The orator Lycurgus' *Apologismos* was certainly
authentic, just as Demetrius of Phalerum's apology for his
ten years of rule was authentic. Some kings wrote their
memoirs. We know that *Hypomnemata* are attributed to
Pyrrhus (*FGrHist* 229). What Pausanias wrote in 1.12.2 seems
to me to refer to these memoirs, *pace* Jacoby (*FGrHist*
159T1). "There are books written by men of no renown as
historians, entitled 'Memoirs.' When I read these I marvelled
greatly both at the personal bravery of Pyrrhus in battle, and
also at the forethought he displayed whenever a contest was
imminent" (transl. W. H. S. Jones). Later, Aratus wrote an
autobiography in many books which—to judge from Polybius and Plutarch, who used them—must have been a fairly
full account of military and diplomatic events (*FGrHist*
231).

Of course, not all the historical *Hypomnemata* we meet in
the Hellenistic world can be treated as personal memoirs.
Some were *Ephemerides*; that is, court or business diaries of
kings and their employees, which were used by later histori-

---

[23] Wilamowitz, *Intern. Wochenschrift* 1907, 1105; F. Leo, *Geschichte der
römischen Literatur* I (1913) 342. As E. Fraenkel wrote to me (24 Feb. 1968),
Leo "had not forgotten Aratos and the other Greek writers of autobiography,
but, as it sometimes happened to him, he drew perhaps too sharp a dividing
line between what he regarded as different literary γένη."

ans.[24] I leave aside Alexander's *Ephemerides*, which have recently come under fire.[25]

A journal of the Ptolemies is mentioned in Aristeas' letter (298). The journal of the Macedonian kings is mentioned by Polyaenus (*Stratagems* 4.6.2) and less clearly by Polybius (18.33.3). At least one ancient reader found this journal delightful, like an authentic book of personal recollections. Lucian, if he is the author of the *Praise of Demosthenes*, wrote (26): "I once read the memoirs of the Macedonian royal family which gave me such delight at the time that I made a special point of acquiring the book. Now I've just remembered I have it at home. In addition to giving details of Antipater's activities at home, it describes his dealings with Demosthenes, which I think you'd be specially interested in hearing" (transl. M. D. MacLeod). It is clear from this that the difference between a book of personal recollections—a real autobiography—and an official diary was not always profound.

There can be no doubt about the private, almost intimate, character of the *Hypomnemata* by Ptolemy VIII Euergetes II in twenty-four books (*FGrHist* 234). Athenaeus read these memoirs, and the extracts he produced do not necessarily reflect the most serious interests of the king who had the distinction of having been taught by Aristarchus. There are details of how Egyptian soldiers picked artichokes and offered them to the king after having stripped off the prickles (2.71). There is an excerpt from the description of the royal zoo of Alexandria, from which it is evident (as Athenaeus remarks, 14.654) that the most illustrious king had never so much as

[24] For the various meanings of *hypomnema*, F. Bömer, "Der Commentarius," *Hermes* 81 (1953) 210–250; E. G. Turner, *Greek Papyri* (1968) 112–124; R. Pfeiffer, *History of Classical Scholarship*, 29, 224f. On the difference between *hypomnemata* and highly finished literary compositions, see Arrian in Epictetus *Praef.* 2, Lucian *De conscr. hist.* 16 and 48. On *hypomnemata* as sources of history, Polyb. 12.25e. The pioneer work was done by U. Wilcken, *Philologus* 53 (1894) 80–126.

[25] A. E. Samuel, *Historia* 14 (1965) 1–12, on a possible Babylonian model for the record of Alexander's last days.

tasted a pheasant, "but if he had seen that each one of us today has a whole pheasant served to us besides the food already consumed, he would have filled up another book to add to the famous stories in his commentaries now consisting of twenty-four books." Ptolemy VIII gave the names of the mistresses of his great ancestor Ptolemy Philadelphus (13.576e). He reported the question that his neighbour Masinissa, the king of Mauretania, had asked the men who liked pet animals: "In your country, gentlemen, do not the women bear children?" (12.518). And finally we have from him the famous description of how young Antiochus IV Epiphanes, his contemporary, behaved when he was a hostage in Rome (10.438d).[26]

We must assume that Nicolaus Damascenus' autobiography, though written under Augustus, was in the Hellenistic tradition. Its extensive fragments present a peculiar combination of a factual account with an apologetic self-portrait. As we have said, he tried to show that he lived according to Peripatetic ethics. On the other hand, he provided a great deal of information on political events, presumably to confirm and supplement his biography of Augustus and to correct the memoirs of Herodes, which he had previously helped to write.

The autobiographical letter, too, must have survived in the Hellenistic period. Apart from Timonidas' letter to Speusippus on the expedition of Dio to Syracuse, we know of Alexander's letters to his mother, which included, for instance, information about his expedition to India (Arrian 6.1.4). We also hear of letters by Antipater (Cicero *De officiis* 2.14.48) and the first Ptolemy (Lucian *Pro lapsu* 10). Perhaps the Macedonians took a liking to this genre. If Scipio Africanus Major, the great philhellenist, wrote an autobiographical letter to Philip of Macedon about his own military exploits in

---

26 W. Otto and H. Bengtson, "Zur Geschichte des Niederganges des Ptolemäerreiches," *Abhandl. Bayer. Akad.* 17 (1938), give the historical background. Pfeiffer, *History of Classical Scholarship*, 212.

Spain (Polybius 10.9.3), he was obviously continuing a Hellenistic tradition, however little we know about it. It was the literary device still used centuries later by the Emperor Julian in his letter to the Boulé and the Demos of Athens.

I shall not discuss whether the memoirs of Aesop are a Roman or a Hellenistic forgery; they are mentioned by the *Suda* (s.v. Αἴσωπος Σάμιος). Nor shall I dwell on that interesting variety of autobiography, the autobiography of gods. Diodorus knows that at Nysa in Arabia there were short autobiographies of Isis and Osiris (1.27.3). These were aretalogies of the type actually found in extant inscriptions (Kaibel, *Epigrammata Graeca* 1028; *IG* XII 5.1.739).[27] Lactantius states that Euhemerus had been able to see with his own eyes in the temple of Jupiter Triphylius the autobiography of Jupiter himself: "in qua columna sua gesta perscripsit, ut monumentum posteris esset rerum suarum" (*Divinae Institutiones* 1.11.33).[28]

Gods do what kings do. There must be a link between Jupiter's *res gestae*, which Euhemerus claimed to have seen, and Augustus' *res gestae*. Autobiographical royal inscriptions were not absent in the Hellenistic age: compare for instance the inscription of Ptolemy Euergetes I, the text of which is preserved by Cosmas Indicopleustes (*OGIS* 54), and those of Antiochus I of Commagene (*OGIS* 383). Augustus' *res gestae,* however, cannot be one-sidedly traced back to Hellenistic models. There is a Roman component in the *res gestae* which goes back to Roman triumphal inscriptions. The Hellenistic precedents, such as they are, of the *res gestae* were given new validity by Wilamowitz when he called attention as early as in 1886 to the similarity between the *res gestae* of Augustus and the inscription set up by Hadrian in Athens which is summarized by Pausanias 1.5.5.[29] Hadrian must have followed

[27] D. Müller, *Aegypten und die griech. Isis-Aretalogien* (1961).
[28] F. Jacoby, *RE* VI 963.
[29] Wilamowitz, *Hermes* 21 (1886) 623–627, partially criticized by Mommsen, *Hist. Zeitschrift* 57 (1887) 385–397 = *Ges. Schriften* IV 247–258. W. Steidle, *Sueton und die antike Biographie,* 178–184, gives more recent literature.

Hellenistic, rather than Roman, models for his inscription. More remote pre-Hellenistic (oriental) models need not concern us here.

As F. Jacoby said (*FGrHist* II D pp. 639–640), there is no parallel in the Greek and Hellenistic worlds to the abundance of *Commentarii de vita sua* written by Romans during the Republic and the Empire, including the emperors themselves from Caesar to Septimius Severus. Jacoby, however, implicitly rebuking Leo and Wilamowitz, added that autobiography was a characteristic, but not an independent, product of the Romans. The confirmation of this is that the Romans felt free to write autobiographical letters to Greeks and Macedonians. Another Scipio, P. Cornelius Scipio Nasica, wrote to a Hellenistic king, explaining the war against Perseus (Plutarch *Aemilius Paulus* 15). Then the Romans began to write autobiographical letters to other Romans. Gaius Gracchus wrote a letter or *hypomnema* to M. Pomponius about his father, his brother, and presumably himself which contained the famous account of Tiberius' journey through Etruria (Plutarch *Tiberius Gracchus* 8).[30] Q. Lutatius Catulus prepared a commentary on his consulate of 102 and his proconsulate of 101 B.C., during which he and Marius had defeated the Cimbri at Vercellae. He sent it to his friend, the poet A. Furius, perhaps to have it turned into poetry. Not by chance, Cicero observed that it was written "molli et Xenophonteo genere sermonis"(*Brutus* 35.132).[31] We are in a Greek tradition. On the other hand, Aratus' autobiography was probably the predecessor of the memoirs of P. Rutilius Rufus consul 105 B.C. and of M. Aemilius Scaurus consul 115 B.C. About the latter, Cicero sadly remarked: "Sane utiles, quos nemo legit" (*Brutus* 29.112). Sulla's *res gestae*, the only one of these

---

[30] On the literary genre and the contents of Gaius Gracchus' work we are not sufficiently informed: cf. H. Peter, *Historicorum Romanorum Reliquiae* I (2nd ed. 1914, reprint 1967), p. CLXXIX; P. Fraccaro, *Studi sull'età dei Gracchi* I (1914) 31; F. Münzer, *RE* II A 1375.

[31] This work is likely to be identical with the "Catuli literae" mentioned by Fronto, *Epist.*, p. 120 van den Hout: F. Muenzer, *RE* XIII 2075, but see the different opinion of C. Cichorius, *Römische Studien* (1922) 102.

Republican autobiographies to be more than a title to us, conformed to Greek patterns in saying little about private life and much about political struggles and warfare.[32]

The Roman elements of these autobiographies are hardly discernible in the meagre fragments. We learn from Tacitus (*Agricola* 1.3) that not arrogance but reasonable trust in themselves had led Rutilius and Scaurus to write their own memoirs. We catch just a glimpse of Sulla's superstition and belief in "fortuna." Sulla claimed divine protection and portents in his favour to assert his right to rule: so did Augustus later on in his lost autobiography (not to be confused with his *res gestae*). A touch of "charismatic" self-display may well have been a characteristic feature of early Roman autobiographies.

The display of ancestors, the funeral orations, the strong family bias of the annalists must have had their counterpart in the biographies and the autobiographies of Republican Rome, but the evidence is poor.[33] More particularly, Roman aristocratic taste for autobiography is perhaps connected with that peculiar Roman phenomenon: the realistic (or "veristic") portrait of the last century of the Roman Republic. The artists who made such portraits were almost certainly Greek, but they had to take into account the Roman tradition of "imagines maiorum" (wax portraits of ancestors), and even more the desire of the Roman patrons themselves to be represented as practical men with wrinkles and warts. Autobiography as a type of self-exposure may well have something

[32] General information in E. Norden, *Die römische Literatur* (4th ed. 1952) 140–141, and E. Badian, in *Latin Historians*, ed. T. A. Dorey (1966) 23–26. The ancient evidence in H. Peter, *Historicorum Romanorum Reliquiae* I (2nd ed. 1914, reprint 1967). On Sulla's autobiography F. Leo, *Ausgewählte Kleine Schriften* I (1960) 252 (from *Hermes* 49 [1914] 164); I. Calabi, *Memorie Accad. Lincei* 8, 3, 5 (1950) 245–302. On Sulla's "fortuna" or "felicitas" see chiefly Plutarch *Sulla* 6. I wonder whether such reflections about oneself were unknown to Greek autobiographies: a subtle discussion in H. Erkell, *Augustus, Felicitas, Fortuna* (1952) 43–128. The appendix to Peter's *Reliquiae*, reprint 1967, gives new bibliography.

[33] Cf. R. E. Smith, "Plutarch's Biographical Sources in the Roman Lives," *Class. Quart.* 34 (1940) 1–10; L. Ferrero, *Rerum Scriptor* (1962) 65–78.

to do with that other type of self-exposure, realistic portraiture. Yet the connection between Roman literature and Roman portraiture is a subject for dangerous speculations; and the very origin of the Roman realistic portrait is a notorious bone of contention.[34]

One fact, however, may be significant in this respect. There is even less possibility of separating autobiography from biography among the Romans than among the Greeks. If modesty about oneself existed only within narrow limits in Rome, modesty about one's own family simply did not exist at all. Republican tradition had consciously been built up on the "exempla maiorum." Roman aristocrats, with few, albeit notable, exceptions, preferred having ancestors in the Fasti to ancestors on Olympus. Aristocrats wrote their lives for the benefit of their descendants, just as they wrote about their own ancestors for personal benefit. If an aristocrat did not think enough about his own glory, "clientes" would do it for him. The Romans were in no danger of having their biographies written by their widows—you will remember Edmund Gosse's lament "The Widow is the worst of all the diseases of biography. She is the triumph of the unfittest."[35] The Romans had their friends and *liberti* to take charge of their autobiographical materials. Sulla's autobiography was completed and edited by his *libertus* Cornelius Epicadus; L. Voltacilius Pitholaus wrote the biographies of his patrons Cn. Pompeius Strabo and Cn. Pompeius Magnus (Suetonius *De grammaticis* 12 and 27). Cicero, who later had his biography written by his *libertus* Tiro (Asconius, p. 48 Clark), sent to Atticus his memorandum on his own consulate (*ad Atticum* 1.19.10; 2.1.1).

[34] Cf. O. Vessberg, *Studien zur Kunstgeschichte der römischen Republik* I (1941); B. Schweitzer, *Die Bildniskunst der römischen Republik* (1948); H. Bouchery, *Gentse Bijdragen tot de Kunstgeschiedenis* 12 (1949–1950) 197–223; G. M. A. Richter, *Proc. Amer. Philosoph. Soc.* 95 (1951) 184; R. Bianchi Bandinelli, *Archeologia e Cultura* (1961) 172–188; V. Poulsen, *Les portraits romains* I, Catalogue of the Ny Carlsberg Glyptothèque of Copenhagen (1962).

[35] *Anglo-Saxon Review* 8 (1901) 205–206.

The feeling that biography is a pillar of the community had not been extraneous to Greek philosophic schools: Peripatetics industriously wrote about Socratics at large. In Rome biography was turned to the advantage of the aristocratic establishment. During the dictatorship of Julius Caesar it became the expression of the most complex attitudes of the ruling class towards Roman and foreign (mainly Greek) values.

St. Jerome considered Varro, Santra, and Nepos the earliest Roman biographers. He probably meant to record their names in chronological order. Varro was apparently working on his *Imagines* in 44 B.C., if Cicero *ad Atticum* 16.11.3 alludes to this work. He finished them about 39. Nepos was still working on his biographies in the late thirties. Santra, whom St. Jerome put between Varro and Nepos, must have been a distinguished writer who dealt mainly with poets and orators. Varro's *De poetis* is irretrievably lost. Only through comparison with later writers, such as Suetonius, did Ritschl and other scholars arrive at the conclusion that Varro wrote brief but comprehensive biographies of Roman poets. We have a more precise idea of his *Imagines* or *Hebdomades*. They were a by-product, with good Hellenistic scholarship, of the work done by Varro in collecting books for the library founded by Caesar. The *Imagines* were planned as a selection of seven hundred portraits of famous men, from kings and statesmen to dancers and priests, via poets, philosophers, historians, and so forth. Each portrait was accompanied by an epigram which characterized the man in question. Learned discussions in prose seem, like footnotes, to have accompanied the poetic text. Aulus Gellius (3.11) mentions a discussion on the chronology of Homer and Hesiod. Two features stand out. Varro placed himself within the Roman aristocratic tradition of *imagines* and *tituli* of ancestors. At the same time he transformed it in a revolutionary way. The *imagines* he chose were not confined to Romans. They were no longer the property of aristocratic families. The portraits of Greek as well as Roman great men were now made available to educated readers. The

spirit of the Caesarian age—with its bold international outlook—could hardly be better symbolized. Pliny the Elder
caught this spirit when he said of Varro, "immortalitatem
non solum dedit, verum etiam in omnes terras misit, ut
praesentes esse ubique ceu di possent" (*Naturalis Historia*
35.11).[36]

Cornelius Nepos developed Varro's notion of biography.
He belonged to the circle of Pomponius Atticus at Villa
Tamphiliana. There he must have met Varro at leisure. In
the circle of Villa Tamphiliana history was a major concern.
Atticus himself did a great deal of research into Roman
chronology and specialized in genealogies. Nepos wrote three
books of a universal history. Then he conceived the idea of a
collection of biographies, comparing Greeks and Romans
from all walks of life and even including a few Carthaginians
and Persians. Foreign kings were followed by Roman kings,
Greek politicians by their Roman counterparts. As is well
known, the only section fully preserved is that on foreign
generals. But we have also two lives—Cato Maior and Pomponius Atticus—and a few other fragments of the section on
Roman historians. The life of Cato is the summary made by
Nepos himself of a larger biography which he had written at
the request of Atticus. The life of Pomponius Atticus represents the second edition, written after Atticus' death. So
many nasty things have been said about Nepos' indifference to
true scholarship that it is worth pointing out that he understood

---

[36] Varro wrote his own autobiography, of which almost nothing is known.
Some bold conjectures on it in C. Cichorius, *Römische Studien*, 196–200: for
possible derivations from it H. Dahlmann, *RE* Suppl. 6, 1251 (mainly Pliny
the Elder). On the *imagines* our information depends mainly on Aul. Gell.
N.A. 3.10–11; Plin. *N.H.* 35.11; Symmach. *Ep.* 1.2.2; 1.4.1; Auson. *Mosella*
305. The basic research is by F. Ritschl and pupils in Ritschl's *Kleine Philologische Schriften* III (1887) 508–592. The fragments of *De poetis* in G. Funaioli,
Grammaticae Romanae Fragmenta I (1907) 314–319. Cf. esp. F. Leo, *Plautinische
Forschungen* (2nd ed. 1912) 63–86 (which is generally important for the Roman
biographical tradition). More information in the article by H. Dahlmann on
Varro in *RE* Suppl. 6 (1935). F. Della Corte, *Varrone il terzo gran lume romano*
(1954), adds little. Cf. now H. Gerstinger, *Jahrb. d. Oesterr. Byzant. Gesellschaft*
17 (1968) 269–278.

the value of Cicero's letters as documents of their age: "quae qui legat, non multum desideret historiam contextam eorum temporum" (*Atticus* 16). He loved to put letters into his biographies: another Hellenistic feature.[37]

Two fragments, which apparently came from Nepos' life of Gaius Gracchus, contain letters by Cornelia to her son Gaius (frag. 58 Malcovati). It is not certain that Cornelia wrote these letters. Nepos may well have been deceived by anti-Gracchan propaganda.[38]

Atticus in his turn imitated Varro in publishing a sort of album of great Roman men in which each of the portraits was accompanied by an epigram of four or five lines (Nepos *Atticus* 18.5–6, Pliny, *Naturalis Historia* 35.11). When Augustus ordered the erection of busts of great men with appropriate inscriptions in the Roman forum and other squares of Italy, he was probably inspired by the compilations of Varro and Atticus.[39] Yet neither Atticus nor Varro nor Nepos, as we have seen, was patriotic in the Augustan sense. They developed new, more international and more humane interests in biography. With Nepos, indeed, biography acquired a new dimension. It became the means by which Greek and Roman men and achievements could be compared. Valerius Maximus and Plutarch are unthinkable without Cornelius Nepos; and Cornelius Nepos must also have helped to familiarize the Romans with the Hellenistic dis-

---

[37] There is a good recent edition of the lives of Hannibal, Cato, and Atticus by M. Ruch (1968). Cf. K. Büchner, "Humanitas: Zur Atticus-Vita des C.N.," *Gymnasium* 56 (1949) 100–121 = *Studien zur römischen Literatur* I (1964) 19–41, 194–196. Cf. U. Fleischer, *Festschrift B. Snell* (1956) 197–208; H. Rahn, *Hermes* 85 (1957) 205–215. Rahn denies that Nepos edited his biographies twice. But his demonstration does not persuade me. Datames' life seems to have been a later addition. In general G. Wissowa, *RE* IV 1408–1417; M. Schanz and C. Hosius, *Geschichte der röm. Literatur* I (1927) 351–361.

[38] E. Fraenkel, *Leseproben aus Reden Ciceros und Catos* (1968) 161–163, is the latest eminent scholar to believe unconditionally in the authenticity of Cornelia's letters: his predecessors include Mommsen and F. Leo. But see the cautious remarks by P. Fraccaro, *Opuscula* II (1957) 43.

[39] A. Degrassi, *Inscriptiones Italiae* XIII 3, *Elogia* (1937). On the *Elogia* of Tarquinia the recent discovery by M. Torelli, *Studi Etruschi* 36 (1968) 467–470 throws new light (with bibl.).

tinction between history and biography.[40] Nepos' biographies were still appreciated at the end of the fourth century. We know the name of one of the learned men who read (and perhaps copied) Cornelius Nepos under Theodosius I or Theodosius II. For some unexplained accident of the manuscript tradition the name of this man—(Aemilius?) Probus—displaced that of Nepos as the author of the lives of foreign generals. Early Italian humanists (such as Sicco Polenton) discovered the mistake when they compared these lives with those of Cato and Atticus, which had remained attributed to Cornelius Nepos.[41]

Surrounded by this concern with biography which he had found in Rome about 30 B.C., Dionysius of Halicarnassus exploited biographical data for settling questions of authenticity in his writings on Greek orators.[42]

Biography gained prestige in the Imperial age for contradictory reasons. Biography was the natural form of telling the story of a Caesar. On the other hand, biography was a vehicle for unorthodox political and philosophic ideas. To write biographies or encomia of Paetus Thrasea and of Helvidius Priscus (as Arulenus Rusticus and Herennius Senecio did) became a capital offence under the tyranny of Domitian. What is characteristic of the age of Plutarch, Tacitus, and Suetonius is that these writers refused to yield to the

[40] *Pelopidas* 1: "Vereor, si res explicare incipiam, ne non vitam eius enarrare, sed historiam videar scribere." The distinction is implied, I believe, in *Ad Herennium* 1.8.13 and Cic. *De invent.* 1.19.27, but the point is by no means certain. Asclepiades in Sextus Emp. *Adv. Mathem.* 1.253.

[41] L. Traube, *Sitzungsb. Bayer. Akad.,* 1891, 409–425 = *Vorlesungen und Abhandlungen* III (1920) 20–30; M. Schanz, *Gesch. der röm. Literatur* I, 2 (3rd ed., 1909) 154–155; W. A. Baehrens, *Hermes* 50 (1915) 266–270. The interpretation of (Aemilius) Probus' epigram at the end of the life of Hannibal, which is at the root of the mistake, is not yet beyond doubt. It may have nothing to do with Cornelius Nepos. On Sicco Polenton, R. Sabbadini, *Le scoperte dei codici latini e greci ne' secoli XIV e XV* (1905, reprint 1967) 186. D. Lambinus in his commentary on Nepos (Paris 1569), introduction, got all the essential facts right. An attempt to explain "Aemilius" in S. Mazzarino, *Stilicone* (1942) 244 n. 3.

[42] We can judge Dionysius mainly from his pamphlet on Dinarchus: ed. G. Marenghi (Milano 1970).

"felicitas temporum" and to let biography become an instrument of Imperial propaganda. Plutarch—so far as we can judge from his surviving biographies of Roman emperors—was no panegyrist. Tacitus wrote one biography only; it was not of an emperor. Suetonius wrote biographies of Caesars which applied to the emperors methods of description and documentation more usually meant to satisfy curiosity about literary men—common mortals.

It is pleasant to conclude by noting that Roman biography contributed to keeping emperors within the bounds of mortality.

Conclusion

Though our evidence for the fifth century B.C. is admittedly poor, the first Greek biographies and autobiographies seem to belong to the period between 500 and 480 B.C. and to be contemporary with the first works on genealogy and periegesis.

One of the spectacular features of intellectual life in the fifth century is the development of a new branch of research: history. History implies an attempt to put order into the knowledge of remote and recent events on the basis of rational principles of source criticism. Some items of information are found to be better than others. The notion of cause is systematically applied to human events and becomes an essential part of their interpretation. Three elements contribute to the new notion of history: doubt about traditional myths and genealogies; curiosity about foreign lands and institutions; interest in the variety of human types, within and without the same nation. But what gives historical research its distinctive flavour and maturity is increasing subordination of genealogy and travel accounts to the critical narration of political and military events—more specifically to recent Greek political and military events. Herodotus and Thucydides are of course the principal names associated with this development. Their prestige overshadowed all other achievements of fifth-century investigation of human affairs. The study of local history, institutions, customs, and vocabulary existed in the fifth century but was less influential and renowned than the study of political history.

Among the less conspicuous products of the new historical curiosity of the fifth century B.C. I place biography: less conspicuous not in terms of future development, but of immediate achievements. The little we know about biographical writing in that century seems to fall, roughly speaking, into one of three categories. There were accounts of remarkable contemporaries; and the accounts might be partly autobiographical. There was research about literary figures of the past which in some cases was meant to satisfy pure curiosity about the individuals concerned, but in other cases was connected with investigations into the nature and meaning of poetry or of wisdom. Finally, there were attempts to put some order into the lives of mythical heroes. We do not know whether some of these developments were suggested to the Greeks by their oriental neighbours. But we must bear in mind that Greek historiography first developed in a region ruled by the Persians. There are some indications that the Greeks knew oriental stories.

The philosophic and rhetorical schools of the fourth century developed the art of talking about individuals, including the most important of individuals—oneself. Rhetoricians created the prose encomium of the individual. Philosophers developed the idealized biography of the monarch and of the philosopher. Both rhetoricians and philosophers used apologetic speeches and letters to characterize a man. It was a development full of ambiguities. Fact and fiction were freely mixed by rhetoricians as well as by philosophers. Plato cared no more for historical truth than did Isocrates. Even historians like Xenophon with a philosophic education forgot about truth when they came to write encomia and idealized biographies. Either because of, or in spite of, these ambiguities, the exploration of individual lives made enormous progress in the fourth century. It covered new ground. The characterization of individuals, the art of portrayal, the study of human motives became more subtle. Great importance was attributed to the formative years of adolescence. Xenophon wrote portraits of generals in the *Anabasis*. Theopompus recognized the importance of the individual as such and put one man at the centre of his historical narration in the *Philippica*. The historians of Alexander the Great followed his example. But biography and history did not merge.

Aristotle realized that careful collection of authentic facts about individual lives could contribute positively to the construction of his own philosophy, and more particularly of his poetics, morals, and politics. He made his pupils do historical research.

Aristotle himself never wrote biography, though he had a taste for anecdotes. It is arguable that full-fledged biography would never have entered the Peripatos but for the strange personality of Aristoxenus. What Aristoxenus learned in this respect from his previous Pythagorean masters, before joining the Peripatetic school, is a mystery. But he seems to have been the first to give biography a new shape. What we call Hellenistic biography with its distinctive features of erudition, scholarly zeal, realism of details, and gossip seems to be the creation of Aristoxenus rather than of Aristotle. Clearly it fitted into the new Hellenistic fashion of care for details, erudition, elegant gossip. Rhetoricians and philosophers still wrote apologies and encomia. But what was now called *bios* was a detached, slightly humorous account of events and opinions characterizing an individual. If the individual in question was a king or a politician, biography remained close to political history. Otherwise it served the double purpose of characterizing an individual philosopher, poet, or artist as well as the school to which he belonged.

Autobiography was not easily reconcilable with erudition. In the Hellenistic age kings and politicians seem to have monopolized autobiographical writing as an instrument of self-assertion and self-defense. Roman politicians borrowed autobiography from the Greeks in the second century B.C. for the same purpose. Members of the Roman ruling class, who were used to writing the elogia of their own ancestors, gladly took to writing autobiography. Biography seems to have reached Rome a little later, in the first century B.C. With

Cornelius Nepos and Varro it became a way of comparing Romans with Greeks and other foreigners. It helped to create a cosmopolitan civilization. Interest in biography was increased by this confrontation between Greek and Roman civilizations. I think it is not mere chance that so much biographical material, both Greek and Roman, has come down to us from the time of the Roman Empire. The element of gossip, of frivolous erudition, remained strong in biographies of the Imperial age. But on the whole we sense a new atmosphere. The writers of biographies created a meaningful relation between the living and the dead. The wise man, the martyr, and the saint became central subjects of biography in addition to the king, the writer, and the philosopher.

The Greeks and the Romans realized that writing about the life of a fellow man is not quite the same as writing history. Perhaps we can do better. Perhaps we can absorb biography into history without any residuum. But we must not be too hasty. By keeping biography separate from history the Greeks and the Romans were able to appreciate what constitutes a poet, a philosopher, a martyr, a saint. They were also able to appreciate what remains human in a king or in a politician. That dim figure, Skylax of Caryanda, the explorer of the Indian coasts and the first biographer, has left us with a problem.

Select Bibliography   Index

A Select Introductory Bibliography

1 GENERAL

E. Paxton Hood, *The Uses of Biography*, London 1852.

E. Gosse, "The Custom of Biography," *The Anglo-Saxon Review* 8 (March 1901) 195–208.

E. Platzhoff-Lejeune, *Werk und Persönlichkeit: Zu einer Theorie der Biographie*, Minden 1903.

S. Lee, *Principles of Biography*, Cambridge 1911.

W. R. Thayer, *The Art of Biography*, New York 1920.

W. Dilthey, *Gesammelte Schriften* V, Leipzig–Berlin 1924.

Virginia Woolf, "The Art of Biography," *Collected Essays*, London 1967, IV, 221–228.

——— "The New Biography," *ibid.*, 229–235.

A. Maurois, *Aspects de la biographie*, Paris 1928.

H. von Srbik et al., "Historische Belletristik," *Historische Zeitschrift* 138 (1928) 593–633 (also in independent reprint).

E. Ludwig, "Historie und Dichtung," *Neue Rundschau* 40, 1 (1929) 358–381.

——— "Ueber die Grösse," *Neue Rundschau* 40, 2 (1929) 83–99.

W. Mommsen, *"Legitime" und "illegitime" Geschichtsschreibung: Eine Auseinandersetzung mit Emil Ludwig*, München–Berlin 1930.

J. Müller, "Dilthey und das Problem der historischen Biographie," *Archiv für Kulturgeschichte* 23 (1932) 89–108.

K. Hampe, "Das neueste Lebensbild Kaiser Friedrichs II," *Historische Zeitschrift* 146 (1932) 441–475.

L. Mumford, "The Task of Modern Biography," *English Journal* 23 (1934) 1–9.

A. M. Clark, *Autobiography: Its Genesis and Phases*, London 1935.

E. Ludwig, *Die Kunst der Biographie*, Paris 1936.

D. Durling and W. Watts (eds.), *Biography: Varieties and Parallels*, New York 1941.

H. Cherniss, *The Biographical Fashion in Literary Criticism*, University of California Publications in Classical Philology 12, 15 (1943) 279–292.

J. Romein, *De biografie,* Amsterdam 1946 (Germ. transl., Bern 1948, with changes).

E. Johnson, *One Mighty Torrent,* New York, new ed. 1955 (original ed. 1937).

P. Kirn, *Das Bild des Menschen in der Geschichtsschreibung von Polybios bis Ranke,* Göttingen 1955.

S. Dresden, *De structuur van de biografie,* Den Haag 1956.

J. A. Garraty, *The Nature of Biography,* New York 1957.

R. Pascal, *Design and Truth in Autobiography,* London 1960.

A. Chorus, *Het beeld van de mens in de oude biographie en hagiografie,* Den Haag, 1962.

P. Courcelle, *Les Confessions de S. Augustin dans la tradition littéraire: Antécédents et posterité,* Paris 1963.

H. H. Muchow, "Ueber den Quellenwert der Autobiographie für die Zeitgeistforschung," *Zeitschrift für Religions- und Geistesgeschichte* 18 (1966) 297–310.

F. Vercauteren, "La Biographie et l'Histoire," *Bulletin de l'Académie Royale de Belgique* 52 (1966) 554–565.

G. Misch, *Geschichte der Autobiographie,* Frankfurt 1949–1969.

W. Hubatsch, "Biographie und Autobiographie—Das Problem von Quelle und Darstellung", in *XIII. Internationaler Congress der Historischen Wissenschaften,* Moscow 1970.

2 GREEK BIOGRAPHY

A. Westermann, Βιογράφοι, *Vitarum Scriptores Graeci Minores,* Brunsvigae 1845.

F. Jacoby, *Die Fragmente der griechischen Historiker,* Berlin–Leiden 1923ff.

C. Wachsmuth, *Einleitung in das Studium der alten Geschichte,* Leipzig 1895.

I. Bruns, *Das literarische Porträt der Griechen im fünften und vierten Jahrhundert vor Christi Geburt,* Berlin 1896.

——— *Die Persönlichkeit in der Geschichtsschreibung der Alten,* Berlin 1898.

E. Meyer, "Die Biographie Kimons," in *Forschungen zur alten Geschichte* II, Halle 1899, 1–87.

F. Leo, *Die griechisch-römische Biographie nach ihrer litterarischen Form,* Leipzig 1901.

G. Fraustadt, *Encomiorum in litteris Graecis usque ad Romanam aetatem historia,* Leipzig 1909.

E. Rohde, *Der griechische Roman und seine Vorläufer,* 3rd ed., Leipzig 1914.

W. Gemoll, *Das Apophthegma,* Wien 1924.

G. Misener, "Iconistic Portraits," *Classical Philology* 19 (1924) 97–123.

F. Dornseiff, "Literarische Verwendungen des Beispiels," *Vorträge der Bibliothek Warburg* 4 (1924–1925) 206–228.

W. Graf Uxkull-Gyllenband, *Plutarch und die griechische Biographie,* Stuttgart 1927.

D. R. Stuart, *Epochs of Greek and Roman Biography,* Berkeley 1928.

A. Weizsäcker, *Untersuchungen über Plutarchs biographische Technik,* Berlin 1931.

H. Kornhardt, *Exemplum,* Göttingen 1936.

M. Müller, *Untersuchungen über das Vorbild,* Zürich 1949.

B. Lavagnini, *Studi sul romanzo greco,* Messina and Firenze 1950.

W. Steidle, *Sueton und die antike Biographie,* München 1951.

H. Gerstinger, art. "Biographie" in *Reallexikon für Antike und Christentum* II (1954) 386–391.

A. Dihle, *Studien zur griechischen Biographie* (Abhandl. Akad. Göttingen, 3, 37), 1956.

K. von Fritz, review of A. Dihle, *Studien zur griechischen Biographie,* in *Gnomon* 28 (1956) 326–332.

H. Strasburger, "Komik und Satire in der griechischen Geschichtsschreibung," *Festgabe für P. Kirn* (Berlin 1961) 13–45.

O. Gigon and C. Andresen, art. "Biographie" in *Lexikon der Alten Welt* (1965) 469–473.

A. Lumpe, art. "Exemplum" in *Reallexikon für Antike und Christentum* VI (1966) 1229–1257.

H. Drexler, *Die Entdeckung des Individuums,* Salzburg 1966.

A. Ronconi, art. "Exitus illustrium virorum" in *Reallexikon für Antike und Christentum* VI (1966) 1258–1267.

G. Arrighetti, "La biografia antica negli studi dell' ultimo cinquantennio," *Cultura e Scuola* I (1966) 37–44.

B. E. Perry, *The Ancient Romances,* Berkeley and Los Angeles 1967.

I. Gallo, "La vita di Euripide di Satiro e gli studi sulla biografia antica," *La Parola del Passato* 113 (1967) 134–160.

——— *Una nuova biografia di Pindaro,* Salerno 1969.

G. L. Huxley, *Greek Epic Poetry,* London 1969.

E. C. Evans, "Physiognomics in the Ancient World," *Transactions of the American Philosophical Society* n.s. 59 (1969) 46–58.

H. Chadwick, art. "Florilegium" in *Reallexikon für Antike und Christentum* VII (1969) 1131–1160.

3 GREEK AUTOBIOGRAPHY

G. Misch, *Geschichte der Autobiographie* I, Leipzig and Berlin 1907 (2nd ed. 1931 reviewed by R. Harder, *Gnomon* 8 [1932] 162–165).

U. von Wilamowitz-Moellendorff, "Die Autobiographie im Altertum," *Intern. Wochenschrift für Wissenschaft, Kunst und Technik* 1 (1907) 1105–1114.

F. Jacoby, "Mischs Geschichte der Autobiographie," in *Deutsche Literaturzeitung* 30 (1909) 1093–1098, 1157–1163, 1421–1423.

L. Niedermeier, *Untersuchungen über die antike poetische Autobiographie,* diss. München 1919.

A. Sixoo, art. "Autobiographie" in *Reallexikon für Antike und Christentum* I (1950) 1050–1055.

G. Misch, *Geschichte der Autobiographie* I, 1–2, 3rd ed., Frankfurt a. M., 1949–1950.

────── *A History of Autobiography in Antiquity* I–II, Engl. transl., London 1950.

O. Gigon and V. Pöschl, art. "Autobiographie" in *Lexikon der Alten Welt* (1965) 414–417.

4 THE ORIGINS

(a) Oriental

E. Meyer, *Der Papyrusfund von Elephantine,* Leipzig, 2nd ed. 1912, 98–128.

F. Rosenthal, "Die arabische Autobiographie," *Analecta Orientalia* 14 (1937) 1–40.

J. Janssen, *De traditioneele egyptische autobiografie voor het Nieuwe Rijk,* Leiden 1946.

S. Smith, *The Statue of Idri-mi,* London 1949.

E. Otto, *Die biographischen Inschriften der ägyptischen Spätzeit,* Leiden 1954.

R. H. Bainton et al., *The Idea of History in the Ancient Near East,* New Haven 1955.

G. Germain, "Qu'est-ce que le Périple d'Hannon?" *Hespéris* 44 (1957) 205–248.

J. Vercoutter, *Textes biographiques du Sérapéum de Memphis,* Paris 1962.

F. Imparati and C. Saporetti, "L'autobiografia di Ḫattušili I," *Studi Classici e Orientali* 14 (1965) 40–85.

(b) Greek

O. Friedel, "Die Sage vom Tode Hesiods," *Jahrbücher für classische Philologie,* Suppl., 10 (1878–1879) 235–278.

E. Reiner, *Die rituelle Totenklage der Griechen,* Stuttgart 1938.

F. Brommer, *Herakles,* Köln 1953.

M. A. Levi, *Plutarco e il V secolo,* Milano 1955.

George M. A. Hanfmann, "Narration in Greek Art," *American Journal of Archaeology* 61 (1957) 71–78.

C. Dugas and R. Flacelière, *Thésée: Images et récits,* Paris 1958.

G. Schiassi, introduction to *Hyperidis Epitaphius,* Firenze 1959.

H. Homeyer, "Zu den Anfängen der griechischen Biographie," *Philologus* 106 (1962) 75–85.

A. La Penna, "Il romanzo di Esopo," *Athenaeum* 40 (1962) 264–314.

────── "Letteratura esopica e letteratura assiro-babilonese," *Rivista di Filologia Classica* 92 (1964) 24–39.

H. Montgomery, *Gedanke und Tat: Zur Erzählungstechnik bei Herodot, Thukydides, Xenophon und Arrian,* Lund 1965.

R. Flacelière and P. Devambez, *Héraclès: Images et récits,* Paris 1966.

R. Cantarella, "Omero e le origini dell' Omerologia," *La Parola del Passato* 112 (1967) 1–28.

5   THE FOURTH CENTURY B.C.

K. Münscher, *Xenophon in der griechisch-römischen Literatur, Philologus* Suppl. 13, 2 (1920).

G. Pasquali, *Le lettere di Platone,* Firenze 1938 (2nd ed., Firenze 1967).

F. Wehrli, *Die Schule des Aristoteles* 1–10, Basel 1944–1959 (2nd ed. in progress).

H. Cherniss, *The Riddle of the Early Academy,* Berkeley and Los Angeles 1945.

O. Gigon, *Sokrates: Sein Bild in Dichtung und Geschichte,* Bern 1947.

K. O. Brink, art. "Peripatos" in Pauly-Wissowa, *RE* Suppl. 7 (1950) 917–919.

H. R. Breitenbach, *Historiographische Anschauungsformen Xenophons,* Freiburg 1950.

P. Louis, "Le mot ἱστορία chez Aristote," *Revue de Philologie* 29 (1955) 39–44.

J. Luccioni, *Xénophon et le Socratisme,* Paris 1953.

F. Bömer, "Der Commentarius," *Hermes* 81 (1953) 210–250.

O. Gigon, *Kommentar zum ersten Buch von Xenophons Memorabilien,* Basel 1953.

——— *Kommentar zum zweiten Buch von Xenophons Memorabilien,* Basel 1956.

N. Zegers, *Wesen und Ursprung der tragischen Geschichtsschreibung,* diss. Köln 1959.

L. Pearson, *The Lost Histories of Alexander the Great* (American Philological Association Monograph 20), 1960.

R. Weil, *Aristote et l'Histoire,* Paris 1960.

H. Erbse, "Die Architektonik im Aufbau von Xenophons Memorabilien," *Hermes* 89 (1961) 257–287.

J. A. Philip, "Aristotle's Monograph on the Pythagoreans," *Transactions of the American Philological Association* 94 (1963) 185–198.

H. R. Breitenbach, art. "Xenophon" in Pauly-Wissowa, *RE* IX A, 2 (1967) 1567–1928.

L. Edelstein, *Plato's Seventh Letter,* Leiden 1966.

E. Dönt, "Platons Spätphilosophie und die Akademie," *Sitzungsb. Oesterr. Akad.* 251 (1967).

K. von Fritz, *Platon in Sizilien,* Berlin 1968.

G. Müller, review of L. Edelstein, *Plato's Seventh Letter* in *Götting. Gelehrte Anz.* 221 (1969) 187–210.

M. Isnardi Parente, "Platone Politico e la VII Epistola," *Rivista Storica Italiana* 81 (1969) 261–285.

6   HELLENISM

U. von Wilamowitz-Moellendorff, *Antigonos von Karystos,* Berlin 1881.

F. Leo, "Didymos περὶ Δημοσθένους," *Nachrichten Göttinger Gesell.,* 1904, 254–261 = *Ausgewählte Kleine Schriften* II (Roma 1960) 387–394.

R. Reitzenstein, *Hellenistische Wundererzählungen,* Leipzig 1906 (reprint 1963).

F. Leo, "Satyros βίος Εὐριπίδου," *Nachrichten Göttinger Gesell.,* 1912, 273–290 = *Ausgewählte Kleine Schriften* II (1960) 365–383.

H. Gerstinger, "Satyros, Bios Euripidou," *Wiener Studien* 38 (1916) 54–71.

H. Frey, *Der Βίος Εὐριπίδου des Satyros und seine literaturgeschichtliche Bedeutung,* Zürich 1919.

M. Delcourt, "Les biographies anciennes d'Euripide," *Antiquité classique* 2 (1933) 271–290.

G. Scorza, "Il peripatetico Cameleonte," *Rivista Indo-Greco-Italica* 18 (1934) 1–48.

P. von der Mühll, "Antiker Historismus in Plutarchs Biographie des Solon," *Klio* 35 (1942) 89–102.

O. Gigon, "Antike Erzählungen über die Berufung zur Philosophie," *Museum Helveticum* 3 (1946) 1–21.

M. Treu, "Biographie und Historie bei Polybios," *Historia* 3 (1954) 219–228.

P. H. von Blanckenhagen, "Narration in Hellenistic and Roman Art," *American Journal of Archaeology* 61 (1957) 78–83.

C. O. Brink, "Tragic History and Aristotle's School," *Proceedings of the Cambridge Philological Society* 186 (1960) 14–19.

W. von Kienle, *Die Berichte über die Sukzessionen der Philosophen in der hellenistischen und spätantiken Literatur,* Berlin 1961.

P. Händel, "Die zwei Versionen der Viten des Apollonios von Rhodos," *Hermes* 90 (1962) 429–443.

H. Homeyer, "Beobachtungen zu den hellenistischen Quellen der Plutarch-Viten," *Klio* 41 (1963) 145–157.

Satiro, *Vita di Euripide,* ed. G. Arrighetti, Pisa 1964.

S. S. Averincev, "Biografičeskie Sočinenija Plutarcha v zarubežnoj Nauke xx veka," *Vestnik Drevnej Istorii,* 1964, 3, 202–212.

―――― "Nablyudenija nad compozicionnoj technikoj Plutarcha v 'Parallel'nych Žizneopisanijach' ('Solon')," *Voprosy Klassičeskoj Filologii* I (Moscow 1965) 160–180.

―――― "Podbor geroev v 'Parallel'nych Žizneopisanijach' Plutarcha i antičnaja biografičeskaja tradicija," *Vestnik Drevnej Istorii,* 1965, 2, 51–67.

―――― "Priemy organizacii materiala v biografijach Plutarcha," *Voprosy Antičnoj Literatury i Klassičeskoj Filologii* (Festschrift S. I. Sobolevskij), Moscow 1966, 234–246.

G. Arrighetti, "La biografia di Pindaro del Papiro Ossirinco XXVI, 2438," *Studi Classici e Orientali* 16 (1967) 129–148.

―――― "Il POx XIII, 1611: alcuni problemi d'erudizione antica," *Studi Classici e Orientali* 17 (1968) 76–98.

A. J. Podlecki, "The Peripatetics as Literary Critics," *Phoenix* 23 (1969) 114–137.

7 REPUBLICAN AND IMPERIAL ROME

W. H. D. Suringar, *De Romanis Autobiographis,* Progr. Leiden 1846.

H. H. Armstrong, *Autobiographic Elements in Latin Inscriptions* (University of Michigan Studies 3, 4), 1910.

F. Blumenthal, "Die Autobiographie des Augustus," *Wiener Studien* 35 (1913) 113–130, 267–288; and 36 (1914) 84–103.

E. Norden, in *Einleitung in die Altertumswissenschaft,* I, 4 (3rd ed., 1927) 83, 88.

G. Funaioli, art. "C. Suetonius Tranquillus" in Pauly-Wissowa, *RE* IV A, 1 (1931) 593–641.

G. L. Hendrickson, "The *Memoirs* of Rutilius Rufus," *Classical Philology* 28 (1933) 153–175.

N. I. Barbu, *Les procédés de la peinture des caractères et la vérité historique dans les biographies de Plutarque,* Paris 1934.

E. Hazelton Haight, *The Roman Use of Anecdotes,* New York 1940.

A. Rostagni, "Note autobiografiche nell'epopea (dai Greci ai Latini)," *Belfagor* 1 (1946) 73–79 = "Elementi autobiografici nell'epopea," *Scritti Minori* II, 2 (Torino 1956) 190–200.

C. Theander, *Plutarch und die Geschichte,* Lund 1951.

K. Ziegler, art. "Plutarchos von Chaironeia" in Pauly-Wissowa, *RE* XXI, 1 (1951) 636–962.

P. De Lacy, "Biography and Tragedy in Plutarch," *American Journal of Philology* 73 (1952) 159–171.

H. Bardon, *La littérature latine inconnue* I (Paris 1952) 108–120, 153–157.

H. Erbse, "Die Bedeutung der Synkrisis in den Parallelbiographien Plutarchs," *Hermes* 84 (1956) 398–424.

P. Treves, "Introduzione a Plutarco," in *Il Tempo di Giulio Cesare,* Milano 1958 (a selection of Plutarch's Lives in translation).

——— "Biografia e storia in Suetonio," preface to *Suetonio, Vite dei Cesari,* Milano 1962.

J. Dalfen, *Formgeschichtliche Untersuchungen zu den Selbstbetrachtungen Mark Aurels,* München 1967.

K. Abel, "Die Selbsterfassung der Persönlichkeit in der römischen Geistesgeschichte," *Antike und Abenland* 13 (1967) 150–164.

T. A. Dorey (ed.), *Latin Biography,* London 1967.

F. Della Corte, *Suetonio eques romanus,* 2nd ed., Firenze 1967.

C. Diano, *Saggezza e poetica degli antichi,* Venezia 1968, 49–69 (on Plutarch).

G. Brugnoli, *Studi Suetoniani,* Lecce 1968.

B. Mouchova, *Studie zu Kaiserbiographien Suetons,* Prag. 1968.

G. W. Bowersock, *Greek Sophists in the Roman Empire*, Oxford 1969, 1–16.

8 LIVES OF SAINTS

F. Kemper, *De Vitarum Cypriani, Martini Turonensis, Ambrosii, Augustini rationibus*, diss. Münster 1904.

H. Mertel, *Die biographische Form der griechischen Heiligenlegenden*, diss. München 1909.

K. Holl, "Die schriftstellerische Form des griechischen Heiligenlebens," *Neue Jahrbücher für klassische Altertumswissenschaft* 15 (1912) 406–427 = *Gesammelte Aufsätze zur Kirchengeschichte* II (3rd ed., 1928) 249–269.

A. Harnack, *Das Leben Cyprians von Pontius : Die erste christliche Biographie*, Leipzig 1913.

R. Reitzenstein, "Des Athanasius Werk über das Leben des Antonius," *Sitzungsb. Heidelberg. Akad.*, 1914, 8.

——— *Historia Monachorum und Historia Lausiaca*, Göttingen 1916.

H. Delehaye, *Les Passions des Martyrs et les genres littéraires*, Bruxelles 1921.

A. Priessnig, *Die biographischen Formen der griechischen Heiligenlegenden*, diss. München 1922.

S. Cavallin, *Literarhistorische und textkritische Studien zur Vita S. Caesarii Arelatensis*, Lund 1934.

A.-J. Festugière, "Sur une nouvelle édition du 'De Vita Pythagorica' de Jamblique," *Revue des Études Grecques* 50 (1937) 470–494.

H. Dörries, "Die Vita Antonii als Geschichtsquelle," *Nachr. Gesell. Wiss. Göttingen* 14 (1949) 359–410.

R. Aigrain, *L'Hagiographie : ses sources, ses méthodes, son histoire*, Paris 1953.

M. Pellegrino, *Ponzio, Vita e Martirio di San Cipriano*, Alba 1955.

——— *Possidio, Vita di S. Agostino*, Alba 1955.

G. J. M. Bartelink, "De vroeg-christelijke biografie en haar grieks-romeinse voorgangers," *Annalen von het Thijm-genootschap* 45, 3 (1957) 272–292.

A.-J. Festugière, *Les moines d'Orient* I–IV, Paris 1961ff.

D. Hoster, *Die Form der frühesten lateinischen Heiligenviten*, Köln 1963.

G. Luck, "Die Form der Suetonischen Biographie und die frühen Heiligenviten," *Mullus. Festschrift Theodor Klauser* (Münster 1964) 230–241.

B. Altaner and A. Stuiber, *Patrologie* (7th ed., Freiburg 1966) 236–244 for further bibl.

J. Fontaine, *Sulpice Sévère, Vie de Saint Martin*, Paris 1967ff.

G. Lomiento, "La Bibbia nella Compositio della Vita Cypriani di Ponzio," *Vetera Christianorum* 5 (1968) 23–60.

L. F. Pizzolato, *Le Confessioni di Sant'Agostino*, Milano 1968.

P. Courcelle, *Recherches sur les Confessions de Saint Augustin*, 2nd ed., Paris 1968.

9 MIDDLE AGES: A FEW SUGGESTIONS

W. von den Steinen, "Heilige als Hagiographen," *Historische Zeitschrift* 143 (1931) 229–256.

P. J. Alexander, "Secular Biography at Byzantium," *Speculum* 15 (1940) 194–209.

P. Lehmann, "Autobiographies of the Middle Ages," *Transactions of the Royal Historical Society* 5, 3 (1953) 41–52.

G. Misch, *Geschichte der Autobiographie* II—IV, Frankfurt 1955–1967.

R. W. Southern, *Saint Anselm and his Biographer*, Cambridge 1963.

T. Wolpers, *Die englische Heiligenlegende des Mittelalters,* Tübingen 1964.

J. Fontaine, "Alle fonti dell'agiografia europea," *Rivista di Storia e Letteratura Religiosa* 2 (1966) 187–206.

M. Plezia, "L'histoire dialoguée," *Studia Patristica* IV, 2 (Berlin 1966) 490–496.

F. Prinz, "Heiligenkult und Adelsherrschaft im Spiegel merowingischer Hagiographie," *Historische Zeitschrift* 204 (1967) 529–544.

B. de Gaiffier, "Mentalité de l'hagiographie médiévale," *Analecta Bollandiana* 86 (1968) 391–400.

10. MODERN, ESPECIALLY ENGLISH, BIOGRAPHY

H. Glagau, *Die moderne Selbstbiographie als historische Quelle,* Marburg 1903.

J. Collins, *The Doctor looks at Biography*, New York 1925.

H. G. Nicolson, *The Development of English Biography*, New York 1928.

D. A. Stauffer, *English Biography before 1700*, Cambridge, Mass. 1930.

J. M. Longaker, *English Biography in the Eighteenth Century*, Philadelphia 1931.

J. F. Otten, *De moderne biographie,* Maastricht 1932.

J. M. Longaker, *Contemporary Biography*, Philadelphia 1934.

J. C. Major, *The Role of Personal Memoirs in English Biography and Novel,* Philadelphia 1935.

D. A. Stauffer, *The Art of Biography in Eighteenth Century England,* Princeton 1941.

V. de Sola Pinto (ed.), *English Biography in the XVIIth Century*, London 1951.

W. Shumaker, *English Autobiography*, Berkeley 1954.

Formen der Selbstdarstellung. Analekten zu einer Geschichte des literarischen Selbstportraits, Festschrift für Fritz Neubert, Berlin 1956.

J. M. Osborn, *The Beginnings of Autobiography in England,* Univ. of California, Los Angeles [1959].

G. R. Hocke, *Das europäische Tagebuch*, Wiesbaden 1963.

A. Girard, *Le Journal intime*, Paris 1963.

G. A. Starr, *Defoe and Spiritual Autobiography*, Princeton 1965.

J. W. Reed, *English Biography in the Early Nineteenth Century*, New Haven 1966.

L. Köhn, "Entwicklungs- und Bildungsroman," *Deutsche Vierteljahrschrift* 42 (1968) 427–473.

A. Fischer, *Studien zum historischen Essay und zur historischen Porträtkunst an ausgewählten Beispielen*, Berlin 1968.

D. B. Shea, Jr., *Spiritual Autobiography in Early America*, Princeton 1968.

P. Delany, *British Autobiography in the Seventeenth Century*, London 1969.

ADDITIONS

M. I. Finley, "Plato and Practical Politics," *Aspects of Antiquity*, London 1968, 73-88.

K. Thraede, *Grundzüge griechisch-römischer Brieftopik*, München 1969.

P. Cugusi, *Studi sull'epistolografia latina* I: *L'età preciceroniana* (Annali della Facoltà di Lettere, Filosofia e Magistero dell' Università di Cagliari XXXIII, 1), 1970.

A. E. Wardman, "Plutarch's Methods in the *Lives*," *The Classical Quarterly*, N.S. 21 (1971) 254–261.

A. Momigliano, "Second Thoughts on Greek Biography," *Mededel. Kon. Nederl. Akad.* (forthcoming, 1971).

INDEX OF PASSAGES

INDEX OF PROPER NAMES

83610

DAT